C000040210

THE CHANGING SHAPES ⌴. ⌴⌴. ⌴

'From Dixon to Brixton'

Compiled by

Retired Chief Superintendent

BRIAN HUMPHREYS

CONTENTS

1.

INTRODUCTION

I've wanted to write this book for a long time, but quite frankly, my inclination faded and I didn't have the balls! Why should I eat into valuable social time in retirement? My golf, bowls and table tennis games are suffering enough due to my age and physical condition and writing such a book was bound to eat into my pleasure and also bring me criticism which I wouldn't otherwise have suffered if I carried on enjoying life as I do today.

As much as I admire them now, I was never one of those principled people who wanted to join the police force as a vocation to serve their communities. I fell into it, no I was 'pushed' into it by my dad who had whet my appetite by telling me that being tall, I would be able to continue my love of sport in the police force.

Ever since I can remember, he used to tell me how, when he was caught scrumping apples, the local bobby 'clipped' him around the ear and told his dad who would then give him another similar clip.

Peculiar that, because when I later joined the police, if I had been given an apple every time my seniors told me the same story... Well, there would be no apples left in the many apple orchards that decorated the green swathes of Herefordshire where I was raised.

So, I'm pretty sure this was a myth, spread with the intention to demonstrate the fact that the police were on the same side as those parents who supported the immediate curbing of juvenile delinquency by a 'clout' as opposed to bothering the processes of the courts. This was the way to instil discipline and respect for the law.

So, the world and our local environment has changed and with it, so has much of the way our police forces now operate. It has often been said that our police should represent a microcosm of society. Increasingly there has been a need to adjust here and there, to encompass a more enlightened and educated society particularly in a much smaller readily accessible world, which was not available to our forefathers.

Quite rightly, our new generations are no longer content with being shepherded into boxes sometimes with lids opened for them by society and those who govern us.

Funnily enough, as I now address what is to be the contents of this book, I know that many of the now, younger generation, some mates and the younger generation of the cops of today, will have similar thoughts about the level of candour of its contents.

If I am to compare the policing in my era with that of my children's generation, then I'm bound to be critical of some aspects even though I shall go out of my way to be positive about the many improvements I now witness.

So why write this diatribe? :-

Of course, if it sold well, I would be paid royalties. I have written many family books not for publication but for future reference for my children and grandchildren. I have also written four books that have been published, and unless you find a best seller, then no author gets beyond 'short term' pocket money in royalties. As pleasant as that might be, that's a consideration which didn't enter my mind until now.

You see, I have always been very thankful to have led a pleasant, enjoyable and yes, an exciting life. Within my career, I was fortunate on occasions to have been in the right places at the right time. That goes for catching criminals and promotion. (And never getting caught – well at least not too often).

With 46 years of experience of policing both, as a warrant card holder or on the periphery of it afterwards, I've been very fortunate, or unfortunate, as the case might be, to have witnessed the many changes in policing that society has also witnessed, but from a different perspective.

It has only been recently when, on 16th June 2021, Cressida Dick once again hit the headlines again in connection with the ongoing investigation into the murder of a private investigator, Daniel Morgan in Sydenham, London: -

'ROTTEN TO THE CORE' –

- **Met branded institutionally corrupt over infamous murder**
- **Cressida Dick fights for job after blocking key evidence from inquiry**
- **Savage report gravest crisis for Yard since Stephen Lawrence affair**

" Oh here we go again" I thought. The additional pages included were full of it. We do not realise how harmful such publicity is to police / public relationships which often seem stretched to breaking point.

Such headlines hurt me, to use the same phrase, **'to the core'** and appearing not long after a BBC documentary, **'Bent Coppers Crossing the Line'** had been screened, concerning the corruption committed by very senior Metropolitan Police officers and their involvement with the criminal pornographer, Jimmy Humphreys. (No relation, I hasten to add). He had been paying them very large sums of money for 'permission' to continue trading filth in the ever-escalating number of porn shops he and others owned in London's Soho.

It was just after these incidents were published that I also began to watch a series of TV programmes called 'Real CSI' which I had previously suspected were about American 'Scenes of Crime' investigators. I was quite pleased that each one concerned a UK Police Investigation about local murders with a heavy bias on the processes involved in their forensic examinations. My jaw was drooping onto my chest when I saw the levels of such disclosures but more so, about how each suspects interview involved the suspect refusing to answer the questions posed other than saying, 'NO COMMENT'.

I hadn't realised how far we had walked down the path of our processes facilitating more and more the pendulum of justice being swung so far in the favour of suspects that an unhealthy proportion of them were evading justice all together.

And so, this book will hopefully be a walk down memory lane with me pausing from time to time to reflect on how I see the differences in the processes involved in the capturing of criminals.

I shall do so, whenever I can, by offering some light hearted instances recalled during the not so serious processes of investigations but one will be able to sense when I do get serious, more towards the back of the book when commenting on what I see as the police being restrained in their own handcuffs and at the same time being blindfolded so as to have them operating in the dark with that pendulum of justice having been swung at such an acute angle, towards the suspects, apparently with the pain of their victims not being addressed at all.

2.

ME AND MY POLICING HISTORY

All police officers have varying experiences of policing with much depending on where that has taken place or in what capacity they were employed. Whilst walking the beat along quiet rural settings, I often wondered whether it was fair that a policeman in Ledbury, Herefordshire (my first posting) should receive the same pay as one in the centre of London or any other large urban conurbation.

So, before I discuss the changes I've witnessed, I feel the need to lay the skeleton of my policing experiences on the mortician's table, so that those wishing to, may dissect it, and thereby consider my authority or right to espouse on the subjects I raise. In that respect, I willingly plead guilty to being by comparison to most, a rural bumpkin, policing in small backwaters whose vocational experiences may not match their own.

But before they lay those charges, let them realise that whatever changes were made resulting from 'bad policing' or not, it affected those policing in such backwaters, probably more so than in the huge metropolitan type forces. So here they are, the entries in my metaphorical pocket book of my vocational history with a few personal landmarks thrown in: -

| 2 August 1960 | 16 days short of my 16th Birthday. - Police Cadet. Admin duties, making tea and stoking the office fire. |
| 18 August 1963 | Appointed Constable in Ledbury a rural market town in a beautiful back water of Herefordshire. |

26 July 1964	Hereford City – Foot Beat work. Cider drinking drunks and a constant battle with small time burglars. Aide to CID. The transmission to Panda cars and Unit Beat Policing. S.A.S boys to help us out when cornered. The breathalyser introduced.
18th June 1966	Married to Josephine (Jo) Williams
1st October 1967	West Mercia Constabulary formed from the amalgamation of the Herefordshire Constabulary with the constabularies of Worcestershire, Shropshire and the Worcester City Police Force.
21 April 1969	Promotion and move to Worcester City – a previously 'City' force with many specialists and no vacancies. Patrol and Desk Sergeant duties. Short period at Droitwich Spa - Patrol Sergeant.
7 December 1970	Worcester County Sub-Division: Rural Section Sergeant based at Alfrick – supervision of rural police stations and policing the villages surrounding Worcester.
8 Nov 1971 to 14 Jan 1972	Senior CID Course at Bishopsgarth Wakefield
11 May 1972	Halesowen. Now in the West Midlands Police area. Detective Sergeant duties in a busy sub division of the Stourbridge Division in the Black Country.
1 July 1973	Promoted to Inspector – Shift Inspector in the Force's Information Room.
3 March 1975	Traffic Administration Inspector- Force HQ.
14 April 1975	Inspector, Deputy Sub Divisional Commander of new Droitwich and Worcester County Subdivision. Policing of both Droitwich town and villages surrounding Worcester and Droitwich.
29 March 1976	Promoted to Chief Inspector. Deputy Commandant of West Mercia Police Training School / Chief Instructor.
10 January 1977	Det. Chief Inspector of 'D' Malvern Division until this Division merged with the 'C' Worcester Division.
28 August 1978	Chief Insp. Deputy Sub Div. Commander at Worcester, 'C' Division.

5 November 1979	Det. Chief Inspector, Worcester, 'C' Division.
7 July 1980	Promoted Superintendent OSS. (Officially the 'Operational Support Services' Unofficially the Odds and Sods Section) – Public Order, Riot Policing, Mutual Aid, Royal and VIP Visits, Contingency Planning, Protective Equipment, War Duties, Dog Section, Task Force, Air support, Firearms and Shotgun Administration.
4 January 1983	Intermediate Command Course
18 March 1983	Temporary Detective Superintendent (Long term sickness of post holder) HQ. Force wide CID supervision and Crime Analysis.
15 August 1983	Sub Divisional Commander of Bromsgrove Sub. Div. with more long spells as Det. Supt for long term sickness of same post holder.
19 September 1983	Hostage Negotiator's Course - Hendon
1984	Miners' Strike – I/C two pits in Nottinghamshire – two tours.
23 December 1984	Nominated Deputy Divisional Commander of Hereford 'E' Division. This did not physically take place due to below appointment.
14 January 1985	Promoted Chief Superintendent – HMI's Staff Officer - two-year Home Office secondment.
14 January 1987	Chief Superintendent Divisional Commander of Redditch 'B' Division, West Mercia Constabulary.
12 March 1990	Chief Superintendent Traffic and Operations Division. Force-wide traffic and motorway issues but mostly 'Operations' matters – anti-IRA attacks and Task Force, Royal Visits, Firearms responses, public complaints etc. Anti-terrorism exercises.
4 October 1993	Chief Superintendent Force Operations. Now the Traffic and Operations departments separate to leave me with Operations. – IRA – protection from mainland attack. In Force and external Force mutual aid, Regional Police Operational matters, contingency planning, Royal and VIP visits, Cross Division support

	and Task Force, Dog Section, Air Support, Logistics, County Emergency Planning Team, War Duties, Police Complaints investigations, Protective Equipment, Quality Assurance, Football and special event policing – et al.
28 November 1994	Retired to form own Company – Brian Humphreys Operations. (Assistance to the Legal Profession)
1.	Service management of the Automatic Fingerprint Recognition (AFR) team in the 'roll out' project of the first English and Welsh computerised fingerprint searching facility across 37 of 43 police forces in England and Wales. Rebuilding the service model in Tacoma USA and later involved in a 'Proof of concept' of the system for Interpol in Caribbean Islands. (Someone had to go) Later contracted to French company 'Sagem Morpho' in Tacoma Washington State and paralegal work for US lawyers in Seattle.
2.	A Retained Experienced Personnel (REP) for West Mercia Constabulary - as and when required for specialist investigation work, cold case reviews and analytical reviews of submitted crime enquiries and the mentoring of junior police officers.
3.	Service of Documents and investigations for various companies of solicitors.
4.	Private Investigations for the public
5.	Private Investigations and reporting to the Deputy Chief Constable of West Mercia a Review of complaints, structure and procedures.
6.	Part time consultation to a busy Business Park to set up a Business Association within it.
1st September 2003 to 31 October 2008	School Manager of Elgar Technology College for five years until full retirement.

The above 'whistle stop' tour of my vocational career, will hopefully demonstrate my qualifications to make at least, some, if not all of the comments I shall proffer in the chapters which follow. However, I have no doubt that given the rural nature of my policing experience, it will bring a few 'tut tuts' from those wishing to question if I have the right to make any comment at all.

My Police Cadetship

As far as I was aware no one from my 'Secondary Modern' senior school, had attended a university. Many had attended police stations from time to time but not in uniform!

It is ironic that my entry into the Police service was most likely tinged with a shade of corruption? OK, corruption in its lowest form ......but from little acorns, oak trees grow and sometimes, that's the start of a problem.

One winter's evening a Detective Inspector Dai Davies, the head of the Herefordshire CID, a friend of my fathers who I didn't know, visited our home. I had never seen a detective before, and here was the chief one and he was now examining the copy book I had been working on. Good job I never wrote anything I shouldn't have done in the cover of that copy book!

Puffing away on his pipe he thumbed through my book whilst uttering a few non decipherable 'hums and as' until he finally uttered his verdict. **"He should do Mac"**, (My mother looked on in bewilderment. I wasn't sure that she was aware of this conspiracy, and although Dad was Henry he was always known as Mac. Due to my father's encouragement as I outlined earlier, I guessed he had started the 'police thing' rolling and before long I was in the training wing of the Herefordshire force headquarters with about twenty or so other boy candidates, some of whom I knew, had attended better schools than me. We were all taking the entrance examination.

I bet they never answered the general knowledge question 'What is an alien' as I did. I answered that it was a 'Sci Fi' body from outer space. Well how was I to know that it was another name for people from foreign countries? We didn't have many aliens in Herefordshire.

My saviour however, was the Chief Constable, Robert McCartney who I know had had a conversation with Dai Davies because he mentioned it to me. It was clear in a subsequent conversation I had with Mr McCartney that he had been 'briefed' on me and my family, even to the extent that on one occasion, my dad had been arrested by Dai Davies. A fact of which I was completely unaware, and that I was a 'pretty good footballer' who would be an asset to the force team. This was not a description of my ability that I would have recognised, however, he followed up with : -

"If your application should prove successful, would you be able to play left half in the force team in a week or two? "Why, yes sir, of course sir" – ("three bags full sir"!) ---- Well, wouldn't you?

It's clear that wheels had been oiled and all I had to do was play my part, I dare say that the truth would not have gone down quite so well. I'm pleased to say that my dad was exonerated by the Dai Davies investigation, a watch had been stolen from where he was working and he was one of a number on site who were taken in. The real culprit was identified and dealt with, a fact I'm sure Mr McCartney knew only too well.

The General Office

My three years as a cadet at force headquarters was rather a dull affair and it concerned me stoking up the coal fire in the office and making the tea. My proper job was to laboriously write out the pay sheets for all the officers who worked in the three divisions of the force and at headquarters.

With no Excel spreadsheets to use, they were required to be manually written, then added up so as to balance the income columns with those of respective rows. A separate row was required on these massive sheets for each individual recipient of pay in the force. This was a weekly process and as soon as the current week's pay sheets were balanced, a start would immediately commence for the following week. It was also my job to walk a couple of miles into town to deliver them to the county offices so that everyone would get paid.

By this time, I had got into the police football team but eventually, those occasions came along only when they were short of a player. I did however, hold my place in the rugby team as the below photograph depicts: -

HEREFORDSHIRE CONSTABULARY RUGBY UNION TEAM, 1967

Standing: Brian Humphreys, Graham Millichip, John Moxham, Les Davies, Bob Powell, Dave Talbot, Roger Morris, Dave Carter, John Jones and our Coach, Sgt. Charlie Morris.
Kneeling: Alan Howls, John Maddrell, Pete Warren, Richard Hanks, John Davies and Charlie Day

It was whilst working on the pay sheets that I realised that police officers were among the poorest paid in the country, a fact that I probably hadn't even considered when I applied to join the cadets. Thinking back, there was obviously no joy in being a member of any police force in those days, let alone being a member of one of the poorest ones, which Herefordshire was. I was to learn that police officers had to live hand to mouth from week to week and many resigned because of it. For me, the plus side was that you could catch criminals! (And play sports)

A major event which I can remember about poor police pay, was Sir Henry Willink's Royal Commission on 'Police Pay and Allowances' which commenced in November, 1960, and finally debated in 1963. Police strength at that time was in the region of 90,000 officers and costs were at approximately 150 million pounds p.a. The success of a pay award subject of the review was gauged by the fact that in 1960 the year of an interim report there was a net loss in personnel of 500, but two and a half years later there had been a gain of 7000.

Prior to the Royal Commission, constables weren't earning £1,000 p.a. but Sir Henry's recommendation was that they should. The approved recommendations meant that constables pay was to rise by a maximum of 30%. He concluded that 'the modern policeman is carefully recruited and he is properly paid.'

In the 1960s, £1,000 per annum was considered good pay. That was the dividing line between a respectable job and a poor job. A salary of £1,000 would still only equate to a £14,000 salary in today's times when the average salary is now £29,600. (2021) Whilst prices have risen, average earnings have increased by far more than police pay.

I can remember the newspaper headlines referring to '£1,000 Bobbies', the pay increase was very welcomed but not a lot seemed to have change. I can recall someone saying to me, "If you're in the Police, you will never be rich".

Some officers continued to 'moonlight' fruit picking on local farms, or sorting Christmas mail in Post Office sorting offices, both disciplinary offences. While I'm certainly not complaining, it was only the very senior officers who could relax a little and not wish away the days for pay day to come around more quickly as I did during my early service. it was not until the Committee of Inquiry led by Lord Edmund-Davies in 1977 that there were considerable advances in Police pay and better conditions.

It was also my job to take all new recruits up into the loft where 'hand me down' uniform and equipment were stored. This experience confirmed to me that many of them had just been discharged from their 'national service'. Police capes and greatcoats were expensive items and our force being among the poorest, meant that although new uniform was, of course, ordered but not if I could find something from the attic that would fit. I should have been a tailor really! "Inside leg measurement Sir, do you mind?"

I recall that my own cape had a collar number stamped into it in white embossed paint – 111. This I knew had been handed in by Tom Harry Stevens a renowned Sergeant from our Hereford Central Division.

I had seen Sergeant Stevens at Hereford Police Station but of course, I didn't know him, just his loud voice and his fine reputation. He was one of those strong looking tall and upright officers who commanded his presence as soon as he walked into a room of others. I think he had a Yorkshire accent. Somehow, I was proud to wear his cape in later years.

There were seven of us in the general office which was headed by Sergeant Arthur Roberts. The three constables were Peter Devenish (retired as Chief Superintendent), Johnny Owen who played for Hereford United Football Club and with whom I trained when I was a 'ball boy' at the club. The other PC was to later become our neighbour, Derek (Scottie) Johnson a local and PAA (Police Amateur Athletic) darts champion. The two typists were Madeleine Bufton and Daphne Griffiths.

With the Chief Inspector who sat in the next office, these people comprised the whole of the force Administration Department and in addition to pay and personnel, their duties included the issue of firearms certificates and the registration of aliens. (Not the ones from outer space!)

Even though I dealt with the issuing of 'hand me down' uniform, the penny hadn't dropped yet that this small police force of ours was rather poor and so were the cops who worked in it. I obviously thought that this level of poverty was the norm, throughout the country. Indeed, as such, I wouldn't have thought anything about this situation at all, other than in retrospect.

The CID Office

My final eighteen months service as a cadet was spent a few paces away from the General Office, in the CID Office which, as already mentioned, was headed by Detective Inspector Dai Davies who I'm convinced turned the admission key which led me to my career. His deputy was Det. Sgt. Les Jones who also retired as a West Mercia Chief Superintendent. Peter Devenish had by then, also transferred offices and he joined me in the CID office where he recorded all crime statistics by drawing rings around the relevant numbers on stats cards so that they could be sent somewhere else to have holes punched into them.

As an aside, in later years Peter became the Chief Superintendent of our Redditch Division when I was the Superintendent of one of his Sub Divisions at Bromsgrove. He often reminded me of the three years we had spent sat next to each other all those years ago and sadly, as far as I was concerned, he told me that he now couldn't get out of his mind that I was still that same cadet!

The only other constable in the office was Det. Constable 48 Mike Ovens. Both he and Dai Davies smoked pipes which clouded the office, especially when Mike was working on a fraud enquiry which I understood, he was particularly good at. Iris Orpe was our CID typist.

My sole job was to keep the criminal records up to date. This I did on receipt of all of the results of every magistrate's court, Quarter Sessions and Assizes held in the county. The records were kept in a long row of four drawer filing cabinets and so every fresh conviction entailed a search of this system. I was ever so pleased if the person already had convictions because this would otherwise cause me to start a new conviction card for that person.

The picture of our force's poverty also extended to this CID office described. There was just one other plain clothes officer, Geoff Clements who was the 'Scenes of Crime' Officer for Hereford. In later years, he was joined by Ken Hursey and Ted Hadley at Hereford. There may have been one other in each of the two other Divisions and in later years when I worked at Hereford, other SOCOs were appointed. Anyway, Geoff attended all burglaries as a photographer and a scenes of crime officer. His dark room where, he would develop his photographs was a little room hidden beneath the main staircase. He travelled in a little Austin or Morris Countryman.

One of the few exciting times for me was that I made my first arrest as a cadet. An escaped prisoner had held up a filling station with, what turned out to be an imitation firearm. He had made his way to Herefordshire and was last seen escaping from the hue and cry, into Dinmore woods, about half way between Hereford and Leominster on the main A49 road.

It was our cadets training day (about 6-8 of us) and we all happened to be together in the training wing at Hafod Road and so we were rounded up and taken to the woods. We had no helicopter or dogs and although I saw police dogs there, I was later informed that they had been 'borrowed' from the Shropshire force.

Anyway, with no signs of a 'risk analysis' here, our van dropped us off one at a time along this road adjacent to the woods and when it came to be my turn, I thought that I would behave as the escapee and as such, I ran as fast as I could into the woods until I was exhausted. What luck! My tactic worked, because there curled up in a bush was our man dressed in a shabby mackintosh.

I was, of course, more frightened than he was but luckily, I was taller than him and I guess he had had enough. The deep gruff voice I had mimicked probably also helped. He came quietly and we walked back about a mile towards the road before meeting a whole host of police and journalists. I handed him over to those as seen in the photograph below which was one of many taken by a 'Hereford Times' photographer. It shows the prisoner being held by Sergeant Stan Whittle and PC John Young. (The prisoner would have walked by himself but the photographers were about!) Det. Insp. Dai Davies is just behind. I'm the lanky cadet behind, holding my cap and walking with another cadet, John Barber who hadn't by then received his uniform. (Or perhaps we were saving up to buy him one?)

I was so proud to see the Midlands News on TV later that day, that the escaped prisoner had been arrested by a 16 years old Police Cadet. It also featured in our local Hereford Times newspaper. WOW! I was now a thief catcher! I liked it.

Unbeknown to me, this was one of many photographs taken of the arrest which had been given to Dai Davies and whilst clearing out his desks on his retirement, he placed them all in an envelope and made a present of them to me. I was so chuffed as I hadn't realised that they even existed in our office.

Also, although not making the arrest I had attended a dance one night where the jazz player, Mr. Acker Bilk was playing. Apart from his music, he became famous for wearing a bright vertically striped waistcoat which was stolen from his dressing room. Coincidentally, the girl I was dancing with had a friend who, whilst we were on the dance floor, opened his jacket to reveal the waistcoat. The crime was recorded and I spotted it on the crime sheet.

The lad was arrested on my information but Mr Acker Bilk didn't want the publicity and refused to take the matter to court whilst instructing that the lad could keep it as a gift. (He probably had many more of them!)

The only other exciting time experienced as a cadet was when I was selected to be a model for a recruiting campaign. I've commented on this in a few chapters later on but for now, I must add that I have never included the fact that I had been a 'model' on any of my CVs!

I was also selected for an 'Outward Bound' scholarship at the Aberdovey Sea School. This was a month's course and I enjoyed every second of it – well on reflection I did, but it was hard fun during it.

So what major changes in policing have occurred since then and now having the benefit of hindsight, have they been positive or negative changes?

The huge difference of course, is that there are no longer such small forces with similar 'small' budgets. All city, town and borough forces have now been amalgamated into giant forces by comparison and I'm sure there will be further amalgamations to come.

Poverty in the Police

Apart from the concept that police officers would never be rich, I've often wondered whether poverty had a place to play in the police corruption cases which have hit the headlines. (See later)

A close conspirator with 'Poverty' in this case I'm investigating, I consider to be his friend, 'Greed'. When greed sets in, it can really take hold to such an extent, that its power can push aside all other senses of reason.

Police Regulations dictate that no gifts should be offered to police nor accepted, doing so was a disciplinary offence, but almost by necessity, some police officers became gifted cadgers. Cadging became an art but of course, this had to be balanced against Police Regulations, the rationale was obvious but there were unwritten exceptions to this whilst I was at Hereford.

The Newspaper Wholesalers, WH Smiths was on two Beat and it was the officer assigned to this beat on nights who would pop in and collect the newspapers. It was just a matter of showing your face in the warehouse and since time immemorial, someone would appear with two or three copies of each of the popular newspapers. This could be 20 or 30 newspapers and they were quite heavy and bulky to conceal and carry to the Station. Tom

Harry Steven's cape was a Godsend, not just for riding cycles on duty, but for hiding fags, chips and of course, those newspapers.

The Station Reserve Officer who did everything in the Station from dealing with the Public to looking after the phone and the prisoners, would also roast us the equivalent of a full Sunday roast every night. We paid for this and something like two shillings comes to mind. (10 new pence) This entailed cooking for about fifteen people split into two sittings at 1am and 2am. We would be joined by the 'Traffic' car and on occasions, staff from the Information Room at Hafod Road, shuttled down by the patrol car. What a changing shape this has been.

PC 92 Jack Cook was our shift 'Station Reserve' officer, or in this case, our real chief cook and bottle washer. These were positions usually afforded to very senior constables who perhaps had not passed their promotion examinations but who knew what they were doing. In Jack's case, he had developed a problem with a leg and found it necessary to wear a metal leg brace which was fitted through the heel of his boot. The combination of his 'leg iron' against the large stone slabs which bedecked the Station floor, ensured that you knew where Jack was.

Jack was a happy chappie with a broad smile and a moustache. He was slightly scruffy; his appearance not being enhanced by the dandruff resting on his shoulders. In later years when we had been issued with radios, for whatever reason, when he wanted us to return to the station, he would shout over the transmitter, followed by the call sign, "***get back to Jack's Shack pronto".*** If he had run out of milk for tea, he would make reference to us needing to pay a visit to the **'metal cow'**. Where did those milk machines go? I guess it's the supermarkets have a lot to answer for!

We all loved Jack as he would have no hesitation in throwing out of the Police Station, anyone who annoyed him. These would include people who wanted to make complaints about the police. ***"How dare you!"*** he would say. **"None of my officers would do such a thing"** etc. Oh how things have changed. For one thing, if the police station you might have in mind has not been closed then the prisoner handling would, in any event, have by now, been centralised to less centres where designated Custody Sergeants would control the reception of and the wellbeing of all prisoners received into custody. They too, would have a squad of custody officer who maybe civilians in uniform, to assist in these duties. The downside to these changes has meant that prisoners, arresting officers, witnesses, solicitors and relatives and friends wishing to visit, would be obliged to travel additional distances to be involved with whatever it was that brought them to visit the suspects or prisoners.

Such changes would be embroiled into what was to become known as PACE – The Police and Criminal Evidence Act of 1984 which will be dealt with later.

Whoever was on number two beat on nights, would also be expected to call on the vegetable wholesalers, Syd Wright. The warehouse was open all night and they knew that we needed some spuds and vegetables for Jack to cook up. I say no more. I've been in touch with a descendant of Sid Wright's family and they are quite amused.

As if to balance our conscience with offending regulations, the meat was paid for at a friendly butcher's shop just up the road from the police station – mind you, I bet you couldn't find a cheaper joint in the town.

To help out, we took it in turns to peel the bucket of spuds that would be required for each night's roast. This caused me to receive one big 'bollocking' from the Inspector one night. It was my turn to peel the spuds and because we were playing rugby away from home on that day, it was all I could do to wake up in time to catch the team transport. So I hatched a plan whereby I would leave the unpeeled spuds in my car and when we returned from our fixture, instead of going home, I could change into my uniform at the station and peel the spuds before parading for that night's duty. What could possibly go wrong?

Of course, the bus was late getting back and I just about changed in time for the briefing parade. So, my stupid plan now had to change and involved me sneaking into the kitchen (a converted cell) straight after the parade and getting them done by the 'four slices' method. (All four sides of the spuds which embraced all of the peel)

Of course, Inspector Stan Whittle opened the kitchen door and caught me red handed. I had one of those 'hairdryer' bollockings that you never forget. Being off your beat was a very serious matter, especially on nights as the pubs would be emptying. It was obviously a stupid plan but I didn't want to let my mates down. Recalling that now, only emphasises how serious it was because it has to be 56 years ago and it is still planted to the forefront of my memory.

It was very rarely the case that Jack's cooking would interfere with the duties he was paid to perform, but occasionally, he would have some messages to receive and distribute over the telephone. It must be remembered that in those days, the Police Gazette was about the only national publication used to circulate details of wanted persons around the country. There were regional variations of it, one such being distributed from the Midland Criminal Record Office at Birmingham. (Midcro)

It might be hard to comprehend now but in those days, there were no computers, social media or internet of any description. Criminals were often referred to as CROs. **"He's CRO".** In other words, he has a Criminal Record Office number.

Other important messages referred to as 'Urgent Crime Messages' or 'Express' messages were circulated around the country by one police force passing it on to another by simply telephoning their neighbouring force in the communications chain and laboriously dictating the message to their colleagues. The person receiving these messages would need to type them out and pass them onto other forces and to our headquarters.

If we wanted to wind Jack up, just before 'booking off' time on nights, one of us would ring him from perhaps an internal line within the Station and by disguising our voice, pretend that we were from Gloucestershire ringing in such a message. These calls were dreaded by Station Reserve Officers at those times because, of course, the act of transcribing often long passages of dictation followed up by their further circulation to the next recipients, meant that in our case, Jack would be very late booking off duty. I can hear him now **"Oh Christ, what a time to send this, why the bloody hell couldn't you leave this for your relief, I'm going to be an hour getting home now" etc. etc**. Of course, being paid overtime was just a dream in those days and such unfortunate extensions of duty time were thought of as 'part of the job'. Oh what a change that's been.

So, at about 6.10am in the morning, in the midst of a very long 'Express Message', he would be told by his bogus colleague from Gloucestershire, something along the lines that **"it's time to depart from Jack's shack now mate, get on home".** This would be followed by our footsteps on the stone floor making a hurried departure through the main door which was very near the telephone. Our giggles and cheers would be drowned out by something like, **"You Bastards"**! Of course, with that limp he was never going to catch us and he would have calmed down by the time of our parade on the following night. Many moons would have passed by before we could play this trick again.

So, back to the poverty suffered in those days, despite the Sir Henry Willink income boost, this state of affairs naturally produced something of a problem. It doesn't need a 'Brain of Britain' to calculate that such important powers could and would be abused by some officers often with large families, seeking to bolster their income with a 'little extra on the side'.

Having an additional employment or a separate business was a disciplinary offence, as was being in debt. These were offences for which it was possible to be sacked. However, wherever there are regulations, there will be ways of circumnavigating them and a queue formed of those who wished to do just that.

Part time window cleaning, DIY skills and officers utilising their training and skills acquired in previous employments was the norm to earn a little extra. When, many years into the job, in the rank of Superintendent, I was sent on a 'Hostage Negotiator's course at Hendon, the Metropolitan Police training school. I became friendly with a Scottish high-ranking officer employed at West End Central Police Station, London. He confided in me that he was importing Scottish Salmon to London where he distributed it around the high-class restaurants. He reckoned it was a really good earner!

Ex tradesmen who joined the job were a godsend for their charges were very much lower than the real deal. Obviously, you had to take a chance as to why they left those trades! I personally knew of an ex-electrician who made a good living in this way. Also an officer who had been a builder, I estimate had been making a better living from building houses than he did as a constable. Ironically, he was also one of the better officers I had come across despite being engaged in building during his time off.

Many officers kept large 'produce gardens' and hens. The number of sales of fruit, vegetables and eggs certainly indicated that they too, were making more money 'on the side', than they were in the police and their colleagues were only too pleased to pay them a lot less than shop prices.

I recall a steady earner was obtained by a few who delivered new cars from all over England to main dealers in Hereford. The problem was that on one occasion, there had been delays and those who were required to report for night duty were forced to unavoidably park brand new cars in the police car park. Now I ask you, what police officer in those days could afford a brand-new car? In any event, these cars were festooned with the various stickers attached to the windscreens and 'Limited Trade' plates lying on the passenger seats. All this to avoid being late for their 9.45pm briefing.

It was whilst talking to one of the officers involved in this 'little earner' that he revealed that one of the constables at the station organised a number of wives to work in the fields potato picking. I suppose in effect, he would have been regarded as the 'Police Wives Gang Master'!

The Police Act of 1946 abolished nearly all non-county 'Borough' police forces in England and Wales. This left 117 police forces. However, the Police Act of 1964 paved the way for county forces to amalgamate into 49 much larger forces but it also expanded the jurisdiction of police officers from what had been within their own area, to all force areas within England and Wales. Finally, the Local Government Act (1972) reduced the number of forces in England & Wales to 43.

As an aside, the Police Act 1964 also made it clear that police duties must be independent of politics, something to remember when reading my chapter about Police and Crime Commissioners, later.

Police forces are funded through local rates and central government grants. In my time, this was a 49% / 51% split now amended to a two thirds central government grant 'plus one third drawn from local authorities. This left those smaller forces with less manufacturing or other wealth producing businesses far worse off than those forces housed in the busier 'manufacturing' metropolitan type areas. Our fields and cider apple orchards were no match to the rates income enjoyed by those urban and larger forces.

In addition to levelling out the force budgets, the combining of resources and equipment has meant that even without the concept of mutual aid, which is more widely used these days, all forces would have access to any equipment they desired. In these post amalgamation days we certainly wouldn't be borrowing police dogs from Shrewsbury to help out at our football matches etc.

So far as advancement is concerned, my own career promotions are excellent examples of how opportunities have since been improved by the expansion of force boundaries. This and many other factors involved in this change, will be discussed in other aspects of policing later, at the appropriate times.

So far as negative aspects are concerned, the loss of one's 'family' type force will, of course, not be an issue for today's officers because the force they joined will be the amalgamated force in which they now serve. They wouldn't know any difference. I guess it was sentiments of the heart that caused us not to want to lose our small forces to such giant organisations because, 'Big' is not always 'Best' nor is it 'Beautiful'. Sadly, in my view, if one were to catalogue the pros and cons of the small and large forces, I'm sure that the large forces would display far more of the pros than their smaller ones but: -

From a personal point of view, the emphasis on our primary task of preventing and detecting crime, has slowly been deflected to the production and organisation of tons of administrative tasks allegedly necessary to plan how to do just that.

Issues not directly related to our core responsibilities of a constable appeared to take precedence. Instead of being 'out there' , 'detecting or preventing' we were in there, writing about it, or organising what we shouldn't do and how to behave when we were doing that. A simplistic view, I know, but which I contend is very factual. Did we lose direction or has this become a natural phenomenon of our changed ways?

Later on in my police career, I considered that those who had flown up the ladder of success in double quick time, must have, by necessity, missed out on many aspects of 'the job' in their career. I had become Staff Officer to HM Inspector of Constabulary, John Woodcock, later Sir John, when he became H.M Chief Inspector of Constabulary. Here was a brilliant man with an abundance of experience in many different police forces. There wasn't much that couldn't be learned from Sir John but he often called on my short but sharp experiences in the CID.

Despite my missing out on being appointed a Detective Constable, I had made a name for myself during my uniformed patrol days both as a constable and sergeant. I had many good arrests and commendations to show for it which followed my endeavours to make up for what I had missed.

As a 'City' patrol sergeant in Worcester, I was literally on patrol with my shift constables and after getting some experience on the streets, I was transferred to 'Station Duty Officer. Sergeants behind the main enquiry desk at police stations could not be afforded in Herefordshire but here, in

Worcester, not only was it afforded to them, they were honoured by having a crown stitched into their sleeves above their stripes indicating that they were indeed, 'something special' and one above the status of a patrol sergeant.

I had also been selected to serve for a temporary period at the small town of Droitwich, just up the road from Worcester. The Inspector in charge there, Harry Wright had two sergeants to assist him but they were both on long term sick leave and so I took their place. I enjoyed what I was doing there and many years later, I learned that the same Inspector had requested that I become his deputy when his sub division was amalgamated with the 'County Subdivision' of Worcester and he was being promoted to Chief Inspector.

Rural Policing

Having managed to achieve all experiences of sergeants duties, other than that of Detective Sergeant. It was with that in mind, and my previous knowledge of the surrounding rural area of Worcester, that I applied for the vacant Rural Section Sergeant post at Alfrick. My stint there, taught me to recognise that the 24-hour policing of a rural community by many, but not all, of the 'Dixons of Dock Green' type constables was for me, the epitome of policing. I was also aware that due to scant CID resources, rural officers more often than not were left to conduct their own crime investigations.

My own section consisted of five rural beats but there were two other sections surrounding Worcester where other sergeants supervised a similar number of village beats. We covered for each other and so we were policing what was the rural periphery of Worcester. With Worcester being the centre of a doughnut, the entire 'eating' part of it was our subdivision.

I can never pretend that it was as busy as 'city policing' but it was busy enough to warrant the existence of its own Magistrates Court which sat once per week at the Shirehall in Worcester. Also to be taken into consideration was that when officers, including myself were on a day's duty, we would, in effect be on call for the whole 24 hours.

Our Inspector had a separate office in the Worcester Police complex and in addition, one of the Detective Constables in Worcester was designated as our 'County Sub' detective but as suggested above, in reality, he was almost always unavailable, being drawn in with the other DC's in the Worcester CID Office. That situation turned out to be much to my benefit.

I was left with some great characters to supervise, none of which minded if I took charge of their crime enquiries and I always insisted that I be present when any suspect was to be interviewed. (And of course, when the DC wasn't available).

At Broadwas I had the typical Rural Beat Officer in a lovely man by the name of Jim Hesketh. Jim could not drive a motor car, despite an attempt being made on one occasion to have him attend a driving course at our force headquarters, Hindlip. At least he attended and stuck at it for a day or two then declared himself as having failed and rode his bike back to Broadwas, never to attempt to drive again.

Jim knew everyone on his beat and what they were up to. One of the problem areas on his beat was the Sunningdale caravan site at the very top of Ankerdine Hill, a very steep and long hill. This estate consisted of many static mobile homes and became homes for people temporarily 'in transit' but who, in the main, attracted trouble. Jim was often called out to attend domestic disputes in the middle of the night. Having returned home, he invariably would be called out again to the same 'domestic'. He never complained.

Almost every day, he would also ride from Broadwas to my office at Alfrick where all my Beat Officers had their paperwork baskets. My office was, in effect, their headquarters. This was about a round trip of eight miles or so.

He was definitely the 'Sheriff of Broadwas' and the surrounding area which he policed with fairness and dignity. When he died, the respect held for him was reflected in the funeral service with mourners packed into Broadwas Church and many who overflowed into the grounds of it. That was what policing was all about then – respect on both sides, the police and the public.

Speed cameras, fixed penalty tickets, plus there being far less visibility and personal contact, have been responsible for kicking yet other of those bricks out of that wall!

Over at Powick, by comparison, I had a younger constable in Stan Drinkwater. He was very good at his paperwork and a very neat and smart officer. He had a young working wife and I can't recall if they had children at that stage. Stan was promoted to Sergeant and retired in the Shropshire area.

At Leigh Sinton I had the renowned PC Ralph Gwynne. The first thing anyone would say about Ralph was that, in appearance alone, he was definitely the 'Village Bobby'. A large round stomach, round rosy cheeks and a round red nose – possibly caused by a drop of beer now and again. When stood talking to me he would continuously sway from side to side, transferring his weight from leg to leg whilst sucking in large gulps of air between sentences. Every other word was 'Sarge'.

He and Jim fitted this mould very well except that Ralph was probably not as well educated as Jim and he enjoyed a drop to drink, more so than Jim who was also taller and generally of smarter appearance.

Ralph found it very difficult to write reports, so we came to an informal agreement that when he needed to write one, he would present me with all the facts on bits of paper and I would type the reports out for him. In exchange, he would stand behind me , huffing and puffing rocking from side to side , offering a constant supply of cigarettes. It was a good partnership.

If there was a need to find Ralph when his radio was 'accidentally' not receiving, I learned to invariably find him at one of his local pubs, normally around the back or in the Licensee's quarters. The Bear and Ragged Staff was his favourite watering hole.

Following his retirement, Ralph was employed as the car park attendant at the Shirehall in Worcester. Whenever we bumped into each other, he would thrust his thumb into the air whilst shouting, "All OK Sarge". This was a typical greeting used when the sergeant met a constable at an appointed place prior to the inception of personal radios.

The set up at Alfrick consisted of three properties all linked together. The actual police station was in the centre of the other two which were the houses where myself and the Alfrick Village Constable, Des Davies, resided. Our houses were connected to the office by internal doors.

It was during one of these marathon typing sessions for Ralph that he said, "Sarge, it's getting a bit wet in here Sarge". I turned around and the highly polished parquet floor was awash with water. It was flowing from under the office door that led into our house. I opened the door and the hall carpet was completely under about an inch of water, as was the carpet in the lounge. We both splashed about and eventually, I turned the 'stop cock' off.

It was an old and cold building and after moaning about it, the force eventually agreed to install central heating. It was on that occasion; the fitters had left earlier that day having commissioned the system but they had forgotten to put a plug on the end of a now redundant pipe which had been carrying water. Jo was in town with the girls and it had been flowing out of this pipe by the side of the lounge fire place all day.

So with all of these beats combined and with a Sergeant in charge of them also living on the Section area, one can imagine perhaps a generously policed swathe of land within a huge rural area. These were the benefits of policing to the community those officers served, but what a disaster it was when the decision came to simply sell off all of these village police stations. Much more on that subject later on.

I could wax lyrical about the many stories of these days which are included in my 'Life Story' but perhaps, another day. However, the rigours of 24-hour coverage are nicely explained in the following story which occurred when the Alfrick Constable neighbour of ours, PC, Davies and his family were away on holiday and the telephone switched through to our house.

One of the sources of trouble in the village was the Saturday night disco held in the village hall, with its accompanying excess drinking and the ensuing

32

fights. The village special constable, Stan Devereux who honestly, should have retired about a decade earlier but who had refused, nay failed to hand in his uniform, had earlier attended the hall with me and all had departed quietly; or so we thought. I had retired to bed and was sound asleep when the phone rang. God knows what time it was but on the other end of the phone was Tom a local farmer who was a member of our little shoot. **"Those bastards have put a brick through my tractor's windscreen, Brian".** He was referring to the remnants of a suspected band of drunken louts who had by now walked down to where he lived, some 2/3 miles from the Village Hall.

"I'll be there now, Tom," I said and I replaced the phone and promptly went back into my deep sleep. When I awoke in the morning, I hadn't remembered at first that I had received that call. Then it slowly dawned on me but it was so vague that I rang him to ask if he had telephoned.

"Bloody typical", or words to that effect, he said. I vowed that I would catch the culprit and I turned over every stone possible which meant that I got around the local yobs until the beans were spilled and I got my young man. He (or probably his parents) ended up paying for the new windscreen and owing me a favour.

As might be imagined, no complaints were made about my inaction.

Stan Deveraux was one of those legends you hear about; with regard law and order, he truly wanted to make our area a better place in which to live. He was so close to the 'earth' and nature, generally and as a lovely man, I have always regretted not hearing of his death as I would have moved heaven and earth to have attended his funeral. His age had caused his back to develop a curvature and for his own good, I would have loved him to have retired as he was once directed, but he would have been so upset at that thought.

Heaven knows of the trouble I would have been in if the powers that be had realised that he was so old, that I kept him hidden. I think I would have adopted an element of surprise if twigged but his appearance would have doused such a feeble excuse. 'Health and Safety' hadn't been invented then!

(Thank God) But, just for a second, forget that Stan was a Special Constable. He was a member of our community and epitomised what a local person could contribute towards local knowledge and what was going on. He was one of many hundreds of similar people in local villages and now, all that ready tapped information has gone since village policing was abandoned. He was an excellent example of what our village communities are missing since the powers that be decided that rural areas could be policed on wheels.

Another Sergeant had taken my place at Alfrick but he was the last one and it was not too many years later that, in my view, rural policing had seen its last days. I shall later dedicate a full chapter about my views concerning the death of rural and estate policing. This was the sad end of an era which I believed represented a huge gap in the policing of a larger than 'city' area of our country. What a dreadful shame that was and I only hope that this chapter has had the effect of drawing pictures of what rural policing was all about and how that policing shape has been re-drawn out of all recognition.

So it was that following some of my good arrests at both Worcester and Alfrick, out of the blue, our Divisional Commander called me into Worcester to have a chat. To cut a very long story short, I was promised the vacant Detective Sergeants job at Evesham but I ended up at Halesowen in the 'Black Country'. But whatever, I was now a Detective Sergeant and that little ambition had been fulfilled. We had left what we both thought was one of the most picturesque locations in the country living among a great sector of the population. We vowed that it would be at Alfrick where we would retire in years to come. I'm afraid that was a forlorn dream that occurs to most in similar circumstances, which often fails especially when children start to grow their roots in other places.

Having been sent on a senior CID course at Wakefield, we settled down in Halesowen and I must say that I loved the work as a Detective Sergeant and thought of the Black Country people as being a race that worked and played equally as hard. The difficulty I envisaged with my integration into the CID without being a Detective Constable never surfaced after I had led a couple of good investigations. It was, however, difficult for my wife who had two small toddlers to look after with no friends or relations anywhere near us. The pill was sweetened somewhat when my name appeared on the promotion list to Inspector.

This fitted nicely into the time when Halesowen was merging into the West Midlands Force and so I escaped and returned to Worcester where shortly after I was an Operations Room shift Inspector. Not the job I would have desired but at least it taught me a lot about those parts of the force I was not familiar with.

And so, for the purposes of my qualifications to comment on the many policing changes we were to experience, my record tells me that in later years I was to perform two stints as a Detective Chief Inspector and one as a Detective Superintendent.

3.

SEEDS OF THE PROBLEM?

The Magnetism of the 'Big Forces'

It was on reflection that the issues of wrongdoing contained within those headlines mentioned in the introduction, that caused me to question myself as to whether the problems of police 'wrong doings', i.e. criminality, homophobic behaviour, discipline issues and corruption in the police service now exposed or alleged, are confined to the Metropolitan Police and other big city forces"?

Of course not, but I will contend that those problems are more prevalent in them. They are the forces which capture the headlines, and are the forces where such activity has acted like a magnet in drawing attention to them. I suppose the sheer size of such cities and their populations naturally makes way for such departures from our standard ways of life. I just can't see any seedy porn shops springing up in our Herefordshire towns and villages or the need for their owners to cross palms with bad money for any reason.

The effects have not only caused the public outcry which we have all witnessed, but have also caused changes in policing methods in every nook and cranny of every village, parish and hamlet in our country. In other words, the combined mass population has had to bear the same pain.

It is to these larger forces where recruits often migrate from the more rural areas. Even in rural Herefordshire, people were drawn to the Hereford force from the borders of Wales and from many other surrounding rural places where the nearest police stations of any substance were miles away.

The 'Met' and other large forces become the home of many other people, importees from Wales and Scotland, let alone thousands of English drawn from more rural places most of them believing that these are the places to be, the places where the action is and where they can perhaps, gain more experience. It's also naturally a means of escaping from their home areas where little or no opportunities for employment can exist.

I acknowledge that there are also many other reasons why people migrate as they do but I often wonder why a minority of them act as sheep and follow bad practice of whatever type they may experience or whether those influences where they occur, are real or have been caused by what they may perceive to be normal or have seen on TV.

Jack the Lads

I truly believe that television and other media 'spins' affect our behavioural traits, far more than ever we believe. It was as if that what they saw as the excitement they yearned, was only available in these places. I suppose also, the bigger the force, the easier it was to avail themselves of whatever it was they sought to fulfil that desire.

Suddenly the Police Training School became 'Plod' School, handcuffs became bracelets, robbers became blaggers, policewomen became plonks. Yes, the police service had a language of its own which, on occasions, was far from complimentary. In the same vein, it also became 'cool' to take shortcuts to enable the criminals to be apprehended. To many, smoking, drinking and swearing became compulsory habits issued on the day their warrant cards were handed out.

The most amazing change for some, however, was that their bodily functions, movements and habits seemed to require change. Hands seemed to be compulsorily thrust into pockets, with thumbs invariably protruding. Their heads developed sudden jerks forwards and backwards whilst their shoulders remained in the same position. It was as if these pigeon or chicken-like jerks were made in attempting to emphasise how brilliantly they had performed in some function or other, or simply to make a point. These were the 'Jack the Lads' that evolved.

Times were a changing but even then, as they do now, all officers of any era refer to their police employment as 'THE JOB'. It could only be expected that they were very much characterised or 'modelled' on radio and later, by TV programmes. such as 'PC 49' and 'Dixon of Dock Green'.

For those too young to know, PC 49 was a radio series created for radio about an ordinary bobby, PC Archibald Berkeley-Willoughby solving crime in the late 40s and early 50s whilst working on the beat at 'Q' Division of the Metropolitan Police.

In 1949, Dixon of Dock Green was the old-fashioned beat bobby whose reassuring "Evenin' all" became a national catchphrase, often directed at me today, even though I'm long retired. I remember the series well. Most families would be glued to this everyday tale of the community copper, PC George Dixon, who delivered comforting homilies from beneath the blue lamp at the fictional Dock Green police station. The series became almost a national obsession but oh, how so far removed from reality it became.

Criminality in the form of murder, gang warfare, thieving, rape and pillage and any other heinous crime you can think of, has always been prevalent in our society and sadly will remain. The 'Good Old Days' weren't always that good! But whatever their stories revealed, the police were always portrayed as upright citizens for God and country and peace around the world.

But even in those days, such a portrayal was not always accurate. I've always believed that alcohol was behind a lot of criminality but not until considerable water had flowed under the bridge, did we encounter the evils which the production, distribution and subsequent addiction that illegal drugs brought. Changes in criminality will continue to dictate changes in policing. The battle to keep one step ahead of the bad guys will always hopefully, continue. However, that 'step' does sometimes appear to me to have been reduced to a 'shuffle'.

So, these beat officers who once portrayed everything good in the police service, slowly became cruelly termed as uniform carriers, wooden tops and many other derogatory terms all designed to regard them as serving on the lowest rung of the police ladder. This, despite the fact that I was constantly told on various courses that the 'Constable' was the most important rank in the service.

These derogatory terms were as much used by their colleagues in the CID who often regarded themselves as standing on a much higher rung on the ladder than their uniformed colleagues. PC 49 and Dixon of Dock Green were replaced by numerous other shows involving police procedural work. Such dramas of all descriptions of the police and the justice system have been the mainstay of broadcast television for many years now, and of course, they will continue to be.

We have now moved on, even the good and bad cops of 'Z Cars' and 'The Sweeney' have been overtaken, with shows such as 'Line of Duty.' Which depicts the trials and tribulations of officers involved in internal police investigations (AC12) reaching out to stop serious corruption.

These have been gripping serialised shows featuring corruption in the extreme, probably far higher than the level actually occurring back in the 1960s and 1970s. They are well written and exciting to most viewers but how many times have I been asked if they portray reality?

Clearly those asking had not realised that the A10 Department of the Metropolitan Police, developed by then commissioner, Sir Robert Mark, arose because of those late 1960s / 1970s corruption enquiries. To pose the question indicates most surely, however, that in their minds, these portrayals could be reality. Perhaps their thoughts are correct?

What appears to me, to have happened, is that the shows which once portrayed the good cops are now portraying bad cops. The crave for something different has succeeded. But that can hardly be described as 'good'.

The negative aspect about these changes is that the current younger generations will all have a far different perception as to what our police are like today, as opposed to the yesterdays I have described, when the police were not also feared but were almost everyone's friend.

The term 'Cowboys' was not exclusively used in the building trade. We had them in the 'Police' also. I could go on in this vein but what I don't want to do is create the impression that such culture or bad practice would apply to all who joined these forces or indeed, that it was only these bigger forces that were affected. Of course not; I have been immensely proud of the professionalism of the huge majority of the officers I have worked with right through my 46 years of being among them.

It is such a pity that the tar and brushes come out more often these days, however, tarred or not, elements of the public will be drawn to believe that most, or even all police officers are so affected. "There's no smoke without fire" they may think, but even without flames, the smoke which these cancerous growths emit, should be expected to inevitably spread and every effort should be expended to cut them out.

I suppose we have all exited cinemas in our younger days with a swagger after watching John Wayne take care of a whole load of bad boys. "Yep, we could take care of 'em too", as we swaggered to the bus stop; or was it took a flying jump onto our horse?

4.

POLICE PEOPLE

So, who were these people I was now working with? I am quite happy with the concept that police forces should represent a microcosm of society, but getting there is far from being easily attainable. If that's what it should be, then it would inevitably contain at least a very small proportion of those who were the wrong type for the police.

Although improvements have been made in the standard of recruits, the inclusion of some not so bright, had its merits; they were often good thief takers. Although these thoughts are now only made in retrospect, I also realise now, that my very early colleagues were different types of people. They were mostly very tall and well built, wore shiny boots and always smart uniforms. Apart from one or two senior officers and one Sergeant Selwyn Roberts, I never recognised anything like a private school or 'posh' accent or signs of a particularly high level of education.

Sergeant Selwyn Roberts

Selwyn Roberts was a legend in himself; he must have gone to a private school or he was raised among the 'posh'. His accent stuck out like a sore thumb and that in itself was a huge signal immediately identified by the *'Erefardians'* who weren't used to such an accent. (Though born in Cardiff, I was raised in Hereford so class myself as a true and proud 'Erefardian'.)

Surprisingly though, with him being a minority of one, you wouldn't expect him to be able to get among thieves to become a good thief catcher, but he was. He was bright and he gained an excellent reputation as a detective. He became a Sergeant, but never was an Inspector and I can only assume that

41

he had not qualified by passing his Inspector's promotion examination. I don't know, but knowing him as I did, I suspect that he never wanted to sit it.

I recall that many years later when he had gained sufficient service to be able to purchase his own house, he lived in the village of Bodenham which was about nine miles, a twenty-minute car ride from the Central Police station at Hereford. He became a sergeant in charge of rural police stations, much as I was at Alfrick. Naturally, he seemed to believe that these duties would best be performed with the use of a telephone and that as such, he should be paid a telephone allowance.

He submitted a report to that effect but it was promptly declined. It wasn't long before he received a telephone call from a supervisor about some aspect of his duties and whoever it was, was promptly told in the most immaculate of English language in a conversation which went something like the following: -

"Ah Selwyn, I was wondering if you wouldn't mind a change of duties....

"Sir, I most humbly apologise for the interjection here, but this sounds very much like a police service subject that you are about to embark with me "

"Errr ..Yes"

"Well, I feel inclined to say sir, this is my own private telephone and I would rather wish it's use by others would not involve my police duties. I'm afraid that if the subject of your call is a police matter then you must either come here to have it in person or send someone out to convey the subject of your call to me".

Whoever it was on the end of the telephone; who, by the way, was indeed brave enough to telephone Selwyn on a 'non duty' day, will have realised immediately that this was Selwyn having his 'pound of flesh'. It was a short conversation but its content resounded throughout the force for decades and was raised at his funeral which I attended, and posh or not posh, his wake was held in a back street pub in Cotterell Street, Hereford. This less than salubrious location was probably a reflection of the man and how he had earned his nickname of 'HOLLOW LEGS' a reference to the capacity of beer he could consume.

Not only was he a legend, he would be remembered and loved by all who knew him.

Smoking, Drinking and Swearing

So without getting that tar brush out again, it seemed that one of the requirements of being a 'police person' as displayed by Selwyn, was having a capacity to consume alcoholic drinks and to smoke. 'Crashing the ash', especially with colleagues and suspects alike, was, I believe, part of the culture.

Without being trained, we also naturally learned to moderate our language and vernacular when talking to the type of person we addressed. A police officer will need to talk to all types in society, from 'upper crust' to the other end of the scale, that we more often encountered. The brain would quickly switch gears depending on who it was. A frequent user of blasphemy and the vernacular of the not so dainty variety, was the Deputy Chief Constable, Mr. Charles William Wallin. Apart from his second Christian name being William, how he earned the nickname, 'Uncle Bill' I'll never know because he was furthest in my mind from being one of my very nice uncles. He couldn't half fire the bad language your way.

The rumour circulated was, that if he called you Mr. Bastard, which was often the term he used, - "Come here, Mr Bastard, I want a word with you"! Then you were on safe ground. On the other hand, "I say Humphreys, come into my office would you"? Then watch out, you were in trouble.

He swore at us like a Sergeant Major to his troopers and I recall that having gained good marks in my Sergeants promotion examinations, being in the top 200 in the country, I had earned the doubtful accolade of being selected for interview to attend the twelve month long 'Special Course' designed to train our Chief Officers of the future. It was necessary for all my supervisors to write an appraisal of me. Our short conversation started by, "Well done lad, so you've come in the top 200! Do you really want to be spewing out all that shit those posh bastards want to teach you at the Police College for twelve months?"

I knew I was on safe ground and whatever response I gave wouldn't have a lot of sway with whatever he was going to write about me. At least the only respect I had of him was that he spoke his mind.

So far as drinking was concerned, I look back and probably consider correctly that as well as being behind many causes of the arrests made, it might also be a high factor as to the reasons why most police officers would get themselves into trouble. My view was that it was the root of much evil, but being a 'drinker' seemed to be an essential ingredient in the psyche of an 'old type copper'. This gradually waned with the introduction of the 'Panda Car and there's no doubt the breathalyser changed opinions and practices.

Even the Police Clubs which were contained in most of the busier police stations, were forced to close. This lost much of the camaraderie between colleagues. Of course, having a drink before commencing duty was not on but I often wondered whether rules governing such conduct might have been more appropriate than simply shutting police clubs down. It seemed a heavy hammer to crack a nut to have caused such a major change. Clearly, no thought had been given to the camaraderie that would be lost.

My father never spent many days without having a pint or two of beer. I never saw him drunk and have always thought he enjoyed the occasion rather than the drink itself.

Personally, I wasn't a 'goody two shoes' character when it came to drinking but I had a job sinking more than a couple of pints without waking up with a hangover. I guess unlike Selwyn, my legs were pretty much solid, I couldn't take my drink. I tried a change of beer and then I went on to whisky but even sampling small amounts, I could not shake off that headache in the morning.

Whilst not a huge problem. In later years especially in the Detective Sergeant and Detective Chief Inspector (DCI) ranks, as the boss I would be expected to put my hand in my pocket at the police club bar following a good arrest. I had realised by then that it was alcohol 'per se' which was my problem and not the particular type. I had developed migraines and it wasn't long before the drinks I held reached abnormal temperatures because of the length of times I held onto them. No, I wasn't tight and always made sure that as the boss, I paid my way.

Drinking wasn't for me and although thank goodness, I seem to have ditched my migraine problem, I have often been quoted as saying that I wouldn't mind one iota if alcohol was never made. I do enjoy a tot or two on the right occasion and a good glass of beer or cider on a hot day. Cider shandy has become my drink of choice, but I still believe that the world would become a better place if we were to do without alcohol.

There was, however, an occasion when I discovered that the demon drink could catch you unawares without even thinking about it.

The Italian Job

I had been the DCI of our Malvern 'D' Division but was living then in our own home in the Worcester 'C' Division area. The policy was that officers should always live on the area they policed and so we considered that moving to Malvern would not only fit that policy but it would be nice to live in that area in which we could raise our two daughters. It would also provide us with a good excuse to upgrade our home and at the same time, be in receipt of some of the expenses in doing so.

We found a house we liked in Malvern and so I submitted the usual report asking permission to buy it and move there. Normally, such requests would be approved with the 'rubber stamp' but to my utmost surprise, I was called to have a personal appointment with the Chief Constable Alex Rennie.

In refusing permission, he told me that I was to keep my mouth firmly shut (another one who called a spade a spade) because there was a plan afoot to merge Malvern 'D' Division with Worcester 'C' Division, but the plans were just commencing. There wouldn't be much sense in moving house because when merged, the Divisional Headquarters would then be at

Worcester; Malvern was to be downgraded to a Subdivision of Worcester. As such, Worcester would then be where the DCI would be sat and not at Malvern.

Unfortunately, the DCI's chair was occupied by the 'C' Divisional DCI but the Chief made a promise to me that he intended to temporarily move me to Worcester to bed in a newly promoted Superintendent who was transferring into the force from another. His rationale was that by the time he had been 'bedded in', the existing DCI would be moved and I was to be slotted into his seat. I thought this was a good deal which, in any event, would save a lot of hassle because had we been allowed to move house to Malvern, it wouldn't have been long before we would have had to move back to Worcester.

Waiting to sit in Eddie Barry's chair as Detective Chief Inspector at Worcester on 5th November 1979

So, there I was, the newly appointed uniform Chief Inspector, the Deputy Sub Divisional Commander of the Worcester City Subdivision. This was the position I was to hold for fifteen months until my predecessor, Eddie Barry was to vacate the DCI's chair, as can be seen in the above photograph.

There is much I can say about the Policing of an ex-City Police Force as I had also served there as a very young, newly promoted sergeant. However, I must discipline myself not to drift into other subjects and here, I'm talking about the types of people attracted to the police and the demon drink!

This was August 1978 and soon after, for whatever reason, which I have never since been able to fully ascertain, the Italian community in the UK organised a series of Polling Stations for Italians to cast their votes in their European (Italian) Elections. One such Polling Station was to be at the Stanley Road Primary School located in an area heavily populated by an Italian Community who, by and large, were all employed by the nearby 'Metal Box' company. As a matter of record, when the factory closed down and moved elsewhere, the Italians followed it and the community then became occupied by an Asian community of restauranteurs and taxi proprietors.

However, I liaised with the Italian Leaders and drew up a little 'Operation Order' for the policing of the polling station in similar fashion as we did for our ordinary General elections.

At this time, our budgets had become devolved and we always had an issue particularly, with our ability to fund officers on paid overtime. By the way, paid overtime was something not even thought about when I was on the beat. Even now, it was only paid to Constable and Sergeant ranks as those above were regarded as 'Officers' who wore white shirts, were saluted but not thought important enough to be paid for the additional work they were expected to perform.

My way around saving a few pounds was that it would be no great deal if I supervised it myself. Whilst there were many Italians in that area, surely their number wasn't going to be too great that it wouldn't be for more than a few hours?

I was to learn that it was to be a far more complicated issue than I had experienced at our own local elections. For a start the ballot papers were extraordinarily long because they held a multitude of candidates and the electors were also required to place them in some sort of preferential order. The major difference however, was that following the electors casting their votes, they did not leave the polling station but they remained on the school premises having a good old chat among themselves. Tongues were flapping like mad and arms were flying around as Italians do.

The election was evidently a good excuse for all of the local families to meet in one place and they weren't going to miss the opportunity to have a good natter, in their native Italian, of course.

All of this casting of their votes and talking served to prolong the issue. I was getting bored and after walking around the school a few times to have a smoke, there was little else I could do. I obviously made myself very conspicuous but settled down with my flask in a little office which had plenty of visibility through windows into the main hall where all the activity was taking place. I was to learn that the invigilator with other senior officials and vote counters were to arrive from London a little later and I was beginning to wonder when this would all end.

In addition, the caretaker was also getting a little concerned and because he lived nearby, he frequently popped in to obtain an estimate of the time when he could lock up the school. Both he and I had missed the fact that this 'event' would not cease at 9pm as did our UK elections.

The proceedings were obviously going to last into the small hours of the night and on the caretaker's last visit to me, he disclosed that he was a home wine maker and would I like to sample his product?

I was on duty in uniform but not wanting to appear rude and surely a glass of homemade wine in the privacy of that little office could be forgiven? So, the answer was obvious and I suppose a little glass became a few little glasses and during this little session, one of the Italian gentlemen present popped into the office and saw the bottle. He exclaimed something like, "Ah, the homa mada wina; Louigi, he maka ze homa mada wine".

Before we knew it, Louigi, or whatever his name was, rapidly left and returned from his home with a bottle. This started to snowball as one or two others followed suit. All this now sounds as though we had started a little party but I can assure readers that this was done very discreetly and I was in full use of all my faculties.............that was, until I walked outside into the fresh air when suddenly I felt as though I had been hit by a lorry.

My faculteesh wuz now a bit defected (or something like that). I was definitely affected and I spent the next couple of hours drinking coffee and walking around the playground trying to sober myself up. It was now one or two am in the morning and I had a dilemma.

I had always sworn to myself that I would never put my family's future in jeopardy by losing my job through some stupid act. I had knowledge of so many different disciplinary investigations and had witnessed officers losing their jobs through stupidity. I vowed that I would never place myself in such a vulnerable position.

So here I was, a Chief Inspector in full uniform and, despite my very best principles and intentions, I had stupidly put myself in one of those positions. None of the officers then on night duty in Worcester were aware that their Chief Inspector was on duty at Stanley Road School.

I had in my possession a set of radios and could hear what was going on in Worcester. I toyed with the idea that I could leave my car at the school and call for a Panda Car to take me home. But I could just imagine the gossip that this would bring. Could I pretend that my car wouldn't start – no, that was too risky, they would want to start it for me and in any event, any signs of me being inebriated would cause that gossip to similarly spread.

It was because the officials had yet to arrive, that I decided to say nothing, continue to drink coffee and otherwise get my head clear and see what happened. Thankfully, the officials arrived much later than expected and the count seemed to go on forever. It must have been 3am or 4am when the caretaker was able to lock up and, although I was feeling very able to drive my car, I have often wondered whether I would have passed the 'breathalyser' test. That wine was far stronger than ever I had imagined. I met no traffic at all on my way home but even so, I had never concentrated as much whilst driving. Wasn't I relieved when I finally turned the key in our front door? Yes, even though it wasn't the quantity but the strength of that wine, I still had allowed myself to drop my guard. Never again!

The National Service Effect

Referring back to those smart, tall and normally well-built older officers with shiny boots, the penny never dropped until much later, when it struck me that many of them with around fifteen years of police service under their belts, had already served their mandatory two years conscription to the 'National Service'.

The last ex-serviceman to be discharged from National Service was in 1963, so on discharge, many of them were now joining the force right up until the time when I too joined in that same 1963 year. I was always disappointed that I had just missed out on that experience.

So now that I think back and look at the changes brought by the passage of time, these men had experienced (most would say 'suffered') the discipline of their two years National Service. Discipline would, thereafter come as second nature to them, whether dispensing it or receiving it. My Sergeants were nearly always disciplinarians, so much so, that we were petrified of being on the end of their wrath.

There was only one I realise now, who could not have served his National Service because he displayed such a kind, gentle and caring nature. Indeed, his nick-name was 'The Bishop'. He had that 'Bishop' sort of shape and the round bald patch in his centre crown was the final characteristic that earned him his nick-name.

There were one or two places in Hereford where, on nights, one could anticipate getting out of the weather and enjoying a hot drink. It was fine

50

on summer nights because my trick was to climb fire escapes to the top of flat roofs where I could sit and enjoy a smoke. Keeping quiet would often lead to the noises of the night being heard and some good arrests had resulted. But more often than not it wasn't lead being stripped off a roof or 'Burglar Bill' breaking and entering but either the lanyard of the huge flagpole in St Peter's Square being slapped against the pole by the wind or the Chinese playing mah-jong in The Lotus Chinese restaurant, with their tiles clanking on a table.

Anyway, in winter time, a game of cat and mouse would be played, in which the Sergeant would try to find us in one of these coffee stops. It was 'The Bishop' who I spotted trying to catch me in a taxi proprietor's office purposely left unlocked for us to have a sit down, flick the electric fire on and make ourselves a cup of coffee. What better way was there for this company to make sure their office was kept secure?

Anyway, without him noticing, I managed to spot 'The Bishop' creeping around behind me. He was probably guessing right because I wasn't far from turning into a narrow alleyway called 'Harding's Passage' that joined two parallel streets. As soon as I entered this alleyway, I ran like hell past the taxi office around the block so that now, it was me following him. I knew he would have gone down this 'Harding's Passage' and I managed to spot him along it on his tiptoes peeping through the grimy window of the taxi office expecting me to be sat in one of their huge comfortable armchairs. So, pretending I didn't know who was there, I got as close as I could and started to scream at him whilst shining my torch in his face.

His knees didn't buckle but if he had had a heart attack, I wouldn't have been surprised.

"Oh Blimey Sarge, I thought you were up to no good, thank God it's you"! He looked a bit sheepish but we had a laugh. I wondered if he ever twigged? Rest in Peace Lloyd.

Brawn or Brains?

Being in a rural area, there were many agricultural workers. They too were obviously physically fit and although the police force wasn't a well-paid job, it was more financially rewarding than being employed in the fields. The term 'Brawn and not Brain' was to be replaced many years on with the term being reversed to 'Brains and not Brawn. This was more easily accomplished because with the loss of height restrictions etc, came the introduction of personal radios. It had been pretty well expected that our officers were well built and tall because in those days, without these modern methods of communications, officers were expected to look after themselves on the streets, especially in a place such as Hereford where travellers galore used to join the local cider drinkers to spend their wages earned at fruit or hop-picking whatever the case may be.

I had this problem on my Alfrick Section where year after year, droves of pickers would descend on us for the 'picking season'. One of the farms I'm thinking of, had numerous stables in which the pickers could sleep. Pay day was a nightmare as their pay would invariably just keep them in drink until the next pay day arrived.

Getting drunk and fighting in the streets was almost a nightly occurrence in Hereford for similar reasons. I was to discover later that the cells in Hereford were occupied by these types more so than at Worcester, which was a larger, busier city but far more law abiding.

One of the points I'm channelling towards, is that most of the brawn rather than brain officers were more susceptible to discipline problems , a point emphasised by reference to the change made in terms used to describe the Constabularies. They were always referred to as Police FORCES with the emphasis on the word, 'Force'. Was it a coincidence then, that many years later, Constabularies and those associated with them, began to refer to 'the Police Force' as 'The Police SERVICE'? The 'brawn' requirement had been overtaken by that of the 'brain' which nicely leads me on to our graduate entrant schemes.

5.

GRADUATE ENTRANTS

Whilst a good level of education was necessary to join the police, my own example and my early experiences, must have surely indicated that in general terms, it was more of a 'brawn' requirement than for 'brains'. I suspect that in my day, we were on the 'cusp' of changes to come. In that vein, I always regarded myself as partly of the 'Old School' and partly of the 'New Generation' of police officers. As far as I knew, there wasn't a graduate in our ranks and unlike Rodney from 'Only Fools and Horses', I didn't even have a GCE.

This subject is better explained by my disclosure that prior to the 1960's police force amalgamations, opportunities and promotions in forces like Herefordshire were virtually non-existent. Promotions to Sergeant were not expected until maybe fifteen to twenty years' service. This wasn't a qualification; it was purely because vacancies never arose otherwise than the 'dead men's shoes' situation. Unless officers displayed exceptional talents, for most of the rank and file there was otherwise, simply no scope for advancement. By comparison the huge benefit of larger forces was that more money and opportunities became quickly available, as I was about to discover.

We never questioned our working practices or systems because the way we did 'the job' was how it was and that's it, who were we to even debate it? The changes were to become more obvious after my move as a constable from Ledbury to Hereford; and were really emphasised, following our 1967 amalgamation of four smaller police forces into one, (West Mercia Constabulary) many times larger.

The first experience I had of 'Bobbies with Brains' was in about 1970, at Worcester, when a bright young Inspector (Graham) came to supervise our shift. He had been sponsored by the Police Service (I believe) to go to university for a degree; he was a very nice man and obviously, far brighter than me. Maybe it was out of jealousy that I had always believed, rightly or wrongly, that many of these clever people paid for their brains by being issued with a less helpful portion of common sense to balance our skills. I knew then that that was the path I should have taken but how could I?

There was one occasion however, when I came second in the 'common sense' stakes, well so far as Graham was concerned: -

Arson With Intent

Graham was always very exact and proper and what I have to say isn't a criticism of him but in a way it reflected an unwillingness to bend a little according to the situation and apply that little ounce of common sense.

As a young Sergeant, I had been called to a flat in a small tower block on the Warndon Estate in Worcester. On my arrival, I was told that a chap inside, was the worst for drink and going berserk. This was a grown man who was faced with his more than 'middle-aged' mother being married in the morning who did not like the idea, nor his future step father. He had drunk himself into a frenzy about the whole thing. I was told that it was dangerous to enter the flat because he was wild with rage, he was making one hell of a din. If memory serves me correctly, this was his mother's flat but she wasn't there. (A premature honeymoon, I thought.)

The time came when someone had to make a decision and as the Sergeant, that was me! The officers present had already tried to tease him out but he was having nothing to do with that, so there was nothing else to do but to get in there. If he had sobbed himself to sleep without waking up the entire block of flats, then we would have been content to let sleeping dogs lie. This wasn't, however, one of those occasions. So in I went closely followed by

Constable John Davies but flying through the air at a very fast speed, towards us was a bottle of tomato ketchup which smashed against the wall spraying us with the contents. However, his ammunition spent, we dashed forwards and restrained him.

He soon calmed down and I took the view that this was very much a domestic situation and with a tinge of sympathy for him, I sent the constables away and managed to talk some sense into him. My radio was suggesting that it was all fairly quiet in Worcester so it got to the stage when, following my 'big daddy' lecture, he gave me all the promises in the world that he would give his Mum his blessings about her marriage in the morning.

I therefore dropped the idea to him, that he could make us a cup of tea. He agreed and we continued our chat for some considerable time. To be quite honest, I thought I had done a pretty good job. I eventually left his flat for the Police Station with my chest puffed out. A job well done, or so I thought.

Around two or three hours later, I was in the Police Station when a report came in regarding a fire at the block of flats we attended earlier, and where my 'new friend' had made me a cup of tea.

"Oh No! It couldn't be, could it"? - I must have kept my fingers crossed for the whole journey that it wouldn't be his flat but of course………'sod's law'……it was. The door of the flat was open and it was impossible to enter it without breathing apparatus. The Fire Brigade personnel did this and recovered my man who had obviously had second thoughts and had set fire to his settee with lighter fuel. He was coughing and spluttering but he was lucky to be alive. Me? I too was alive but felt in jeopardy of drowning in deep sh**.

I thought it best to find the Inspector and by explaining myself, I would be taking the early ground. A tactic which often worked in my later post in 'Force Operations'.

"What was the point in arresting this man Sir"? – I enquired; even now I could argue the case but, of course, events had overtaken me and in retrospect, I should have felt his collar. However, my argument, apart from it being a domestic situation, was that he had set fire to his own property. **"Waking up the whole block of flats wasn't a criminal offence"**, I said. OK – Breach of the Peace maybe, but no-one had complained. This was an area of Worcester where the peace was unlikely to be achieved at any time anyway!

I knew I was wasting my time. The Inspector was technically correct in law when he directed that the offender be charged with the indictable offence of 'Arson with Intent', or being reckless to endanger the lives of others. He argued that the 'recklessness' and the 'danger to lives' elements of the offence was present due to the location of the flat being in the same building as other similar flats. 'Bad Luck Mate'.

The fire could have spread to them. He was right, of course, and I thought he just wanted to show off his knowledge. This was prior to 1972, when Crown Courts replaced Quarter Sessions and Assizes and that offence could only be tried in those higher courts. Our defendant didn't deserve going through that process, but committed by the Magistrates Court to Quarter Sessions he was. He was eventually sentenced to receive a number of years imprisonment.

This was not only the wrong decision so far as I was concerned, but I can't remember now, whether he attended his mother's wedding or whether he was in custody at the time – whatever, he didn't deserve all that. Graham, the Inspector and I have met on many subsequent occasions and many years later and we still argued about the merits of the action taken during that night.

So, it was from the 1970s that we gradually saw the introduction of more graduates. I won't even argue that it wasn't a good idea because I don't like backing the wrong metaphorical horse. It was obviously a move in the right direction, a move that I should have taken but just like my school days, the magnet of enjoying myself was far too strong to succumb to all that education.

I can recall asking my colleagues, **"What on earth was the benefit of employing graduates in subjects such as 'Oceanography' or 'Environmental Science'?** Of course, that wasn't the point! The demonstration of the capability to absorb all those facts and figures in order to graduate, was sufficient enough to prove the holders of these degrees had sufficient brain power and breadth of vision to be able to organise, retain and manage information.

The police service will always need educated people who have proven themselves but let's hope that we will continue to employ a good helping of worker bees around these 'Queen Bees'. There is certainly room for bright and well-educated police officers in the service who will progress to become our very senior leaders.

Part of 'the change' in this respect is that from January 2020, it has become possible to enrol into a degree course leading to a BSc (Hons) Professional Policing Degree. This can only be a good thing and I look forward to discovering how the options open to these graduates will change the shape of recruitment into the force and how it progresses into the future.

The concept of 'Brawn over Brain" should never have been paramount but in those times, without modern communications and other resources, there was indeed, that requirement. The world has changed.

My only sorrow about our current leaders, a view I readily admit has derived from what I'm fed by the media, is that our police chiefs of today, as bright as they undoubtedly are, have had their voices diminished by the introduction of Police Commissioners. That subject, however, is made subject of a separate chapter to come.

So in conclusion here, whilst I hesitate to endorse a dual entry system of recruitment, I'm at a loss to recommend anything else if all else fails to attract our graduates. I found the following advertisement resulting from a Google search:-

Do you want to change the world?

Do you think differently? Can you work with others to create new solutions to long term societal problems? Can you bring communities together? Do you want a meaningful career that improves the lives of those around you? If you're a graduate looking to make a real difference, our award-winning, salaried two-year national graduate programmes offer a unique opportunity to transform communities while developing leadership skills for life. Police now offer a structured route into policing with all the personal support and leadership development you'll need to create positive change in the world around you. **Join us. Change the story.**

The Senior Command Course Route

Jumping backwards and forwards up and down the ladder of my successes or failures will not affect the reading of this book by being out of chronological order. Some of the changes I need to explain will be found within various ranks and at various times. On this occasion, with reference to graduate entry into the service, I need to refer to the time when I could have been expected to rise from the rank of Chief Superintendent to the 'Chief Officer' ranks. – Assistant Chief, Deputy Chief and Chief Constable. So, being on 'the cusp' of this change, was much later in my career, to come home to haunt me as I had expected it would, for many years.

So far as my ranks are concerned, I had become the youngest in force to be promoted to most, if not all of the ranks I was fortunate enough (lucky enough) to aspire to. The rank of Chief Superintendent was no different.

The HMI Calls

I had been the Superintendent in charge of the Bromsgrove Subdivision which enveloped police stations at Droitwich and Rubery and the Village and Resident beat stations surrounding them. Being not too far from

Birmingham, it was a reasonably busy station though not the busiest. As with other Subdivisional Commanders, we did not relish the annual visit of Her Majesty's Inspector of Constabulary and his entourage.

John Woodcock, (RIP) a past Chief Constable with a huge amount of experience in the most senior of ranks in many different police forces, was Her Majesty's Inspector of Constabulary for the whole of Wales and most forces in the Midlands. His office had been in Wales near his home at Llantwit Major. However, finding that he spent most of his time in the Midlands, he wanted to change location to somewhere nearer to the Midland forces he inspected.

So having been influenced by one of my colleagues on his staff, he came to live on my Sub Division. As far as I was concerned, at that time, this wasn't one of his better decisions because it meant that he wouldn't have far to travel to inspect my stations! Being a local, he would also be able to observe my personnel at first hand and without wearing his HMI's uniform. Would this be an attraction to him? I thought.

To jump straight to the point, whilst HMI's were required to inspect elements of each force at least once per year, they weren't expected to visit the same Subdivisions, let alone the same Divisions, on consecutive years. When that happened on my Sub Division in 1983 and 1984, I obviously suspected that my suspicions about him living on my patch were turning into reality.

Happily, his successive inspections for me became a blessing in disguise. I was wrong to fear them because over the ensuing years, we became friends and so were our respective families. This relationship was not only during our working together, but for many years after I had retired, right up until his death. Creep? No, it wasn't like that at all, which is why I don't mind referring to it.

As past Chief Constables, HMIs would have had the entire management structure of their force surrounding them, to bat off and share many of the day-to-day problems of their forces. Having been made HMIs they would suddenly find that they had a Chief Inspector to head the administration of their region, a secretary and typist, a driver and just two Chief Superintendents as 'Staff Officers'. Quite lonely places compared to when they were in the proverbial chair as the head of a police force.

John Woodcock was very much a social animal and he too loved sport. Our offices had excellent access to snooker and table tennis tables and a squash court wasn't too far away! It wasn't long before we were playing golf and whilst easing him into Droitwich Golf Club, I was once summoned to see the captain who gave me some stern advice about holding two ladies up on the course. John had overshot the eighth green and it took a few more shots before he got onto it. With these ladies behind us, I knew we were in trouble!

Sometime after my appointment he told me that his second visit to my subdivision was made so that he could have another look at me with the idea of appointing me as one of his two Chief Superintendent Staff Officers. Indeed, he was kind enough to include that fact in some later references I asked him to provide. I was a Superintendent then and such a move would bump me up to Chief Superintendent, ahead of some I knew would expect such a promotion before me. I wasn't going to be very popular with them but popularity wasn't paying my bills.

The upshot was that I spent a most enjoyable two years secondment to him in his new offices at the Government Buildings, Whittington, Worcester. I had replaced a Ch. Supt. Vasey from South Wales who had retired holding that same post. Consequently, as a comparatively young in-service Chief Super, I was very conscious of him doing his utmost to mentor me during the whole period of my two-year secondment. He placed me in situations beneficial for my advancement and did all he could to help me, so much so that I can say without doubt that I learned more from him about being a leader and a manager than from anyone else or any other experience.

Mr Woodcock as he was then, was a particularly good orator who, with a wry sense of humour, could talk anyone around to his opinion and above all, his diplomacy was second to none. There were future occasions when drafting letters, I'd rip them up after saying to myself, "John Woodcock wouldn't be telling it this way", and then I would re-draft them in the way I knew he would have preferred.

Sir John, as he later became, was a true diplomat and I learned a lot from those occasions we had been on a force inspection or had otherwise been away from the office. Our first job over coffee during the following morning, would be to discuss those occasions and he always asked about whether or not there was anyone to thank for the activity on those visits. I became so used to this that invariably, I would draft the letters before our meeting.

We were all aware at that time, in order to become Chief Officers, it was necessary to attend the 'Senior Command Course' at the Police Staff College, Bramshill, Hampshire. Such places were keenly sought after and selection was gained following a three-day extended interview process held at 'The Grand' hotel, Eastbourne. He and I knew that I was to be disadvantaged in this competitive process because I was not a degree holder. Nevertheless, he did all he could to ensure that I knew all of the wrinkles involved. He had been an assessor so he knew them all and he literally trained me with past exercises he knew of.

I have always regarded my life as being without regrets. We have been so lucky in the past but my one huge regret, was that I failed at the first attempt to get on that course, and I felt I had let him down. This actually wasn't unusual and candidates were allowed three attempts and not many got through the process at their first attempt. I knew I'd had a close shave because after all of the interviews and exercises were completed, some, but not many, were called to have a second interview with just one of the assessors.

John had told me about this extra interview and he informed me that these were just to be held with those sat on the fence. I must have fallen on the wrong side of it!

This made me feel fairly confident that I would get there in the end. However, my second attempt would arrive following the end of my secondment and before that opportunity came around, I became the Divisional Commander of the force's Redditch 'B' Division. It wasn't too long after we parted professionally, that John Woodcock was knighted and had risen to become Her Majesty's Chief Inspector of Constabulary, with an office at the Home Office. One of his main functions there was to be advisor on policing matters to the Home Secretary.

There were five regional HMIs and one Chief HMI. (I often joked with him afterwards, that he had got there as a result of me teaching him all he knew!)

We continued our friendship and even following my retirement, we were often invited to dinner parties held at his home.

However, it was as a result of the biggest family tragedy of our lives, that I did not make any further attempts to be enrolled on the Senior Command Course. Our eldest daughter, was suddenly struck with a mental illness. Eventually she was diagnosed with 'Manic Depression', now called 'Bi-Polar' disease. I cannot adequately describe what a huge disaster this was in our lives. Tears are starting to well as I write. Everything had gone extremely well for us and now our world had come tumbling down.

It completely changed my way of thinking and in the knowledge that she would be unable to cope with moving to live and work in a different county and environment, which was then a requirement of Chief Officer appointments, long since abandoned, I went to see the Chief Constable, Tony Mullett. I had already informed Sir John and now I explained to the chief that I would no longer be seeking any further advancement. It was then that he told me that my first 'knock back' from the Senior Command Course interviews was probably due to my not having a degree. As mentioned above, this was something I suspected but had not positively been made aware of. I had been afraid of that outcome, but still hoped that I could squeeze through the net.

However, having always believed in 'Fate', and thanking heaven that my daughter now enjoys good health and is happily married with a child, not making that move turned out to be one of the better decisions I've made and fate certainly played its part.

So that was quite a long explanation linked to graduate entry and progression to the 'Chief Officer' posts. I'm sure that many more graduates are now serving officers and represent a much higher proportion of recruits than when I served. However, I'm equally sure that there is still a place in forces for those with just a love of the job and no intentions of advancement. They will earn good degrees at the 'University of Life' and hopefully, enjoy 'the job' as much as I did.

The College of Policing really needs to emphasise that degrees are not totally necessary to become a police officer and that the microcosm of society will, if continued, maintain that healthy balance.

Under a new Policing Education Qualifications Framework (PEQF), recruits will have to gain a degree if they join through the new Degree Apprenticeship Programme. Yes, the need for 'Brain' over 'Brawn' is now firmly made and sadly, I can only surmise that even being at the right age and even with the help of a Dai Davies, I would never have been admitted into the force these days. (What would they have lost? – LOL!)

6.

DIVERSITY, RACE AND THE FAIRER SEX

Of all the subjects I shall comment upon, the aspects of diversity, especially equal opportunities and sex discrimination will probably be the most controversial. Thus, I realise that no matter what views are proffered or preferred by me, my ears will undoubtedly ring loud and clear in suffering the most criticism of the subjects I shall unearth in this book.

I can guarantee that I shall not be that concerned, because no matter what view anyone holds on these subjects, you can be sure that about 50% of others will disagree with them. Whatever, the world is constantly changing and so long as they're my views and I believe in them, why should I be concerned so long as I do so with respect for other opinions

Before I start on these subjects, let me explain that no matter what I say, I have not a drop of discrimination in my blood, whether that refers to race, colour, creed, sex, gender issues or any other subject of diversity. I doubt whether the minority factions would like what I'm about to say, but for them, I have always felt sympathy. Why?

My thoughts are, that however they may feel themselves, they were born into what they've become. I suspect that they have had little to do with choices about the matter or with the environment in which they were raised. It can't be said that it wasn't their fault, if indeed, it is a fault. I believe that it's a 'genes' issue and not a 'fault' issue at all. We are what we are and also to quote a friend, we are here because we're here!! (Thanks Ray)

Diversity wasn't a common word used in our vocabulary during my day; I had heard the word, of course, but it wasn't until long after my retirement, when I had finished working abroad with the Automatic Fingerprint Recognition Consortium, that it became a very important word indeed.

I had been persuaded to organise a business association on the Sandy Lane Industrial Estate at Stourport on Severn and because this employment was for only one day a week, I enrolled in a West Mercia Constabulary scheme referred to as the 'REP' scheme. (Retired Experienced Personnel).

This was a scheme whereby retired officers who were willing to be called upon to assist serving officers with various tasks which were considered suitable to the circumstances and any previous expertise they held. The beauty of this employment was that depending on personal circumstances at the time, there was no obligation to accept any of the jobs offered. Participants would be paid an hourly rate for any job undertaken. I had some interesting jobs but describing most of them here doesn't come within the title and purpose of this book.

I must admit that as a retired Chief Superintendent, it came as a bit of a surprise to learn that not only was I and my family to be vetted again, (I had been positively vetted to be employed with H.M Inspectorate) I would also be required to attend a two day 'Diversity' course at Kidderminster Police Station.

It was on 8th and 9th May 2002, that with many other officers in service, I attended this course and received the shocking news, (so far as I was concerned), that officers would not now refer to their mates by 'nick-names' or any other name other than their proper ones, or the ones they desired.

What!

I wouldn't go as far as to say that I didn't know some of my ex-colleagues proper names but most of them, and no doubt, myself, would be known by these other nick-names, which apparently, many disliked even though they were not objected to.

I can only think of one that I had previously considered was insulting even though I also admit that it brought an inward smile. The constable's nickname was 'Bungalow' and I fell into the trap of asking him what was behind it because I genuinely didn't know.

He started to grump at me and I don't think he told me in as many words, but whatever, I learned that as he was regarded as being a little 'thick', the bungalow reference was not that he lived in one but was about him having 'Nothing upstairs'.

Many nick-names had evolved as terms of endearment or Christian or Surnames shortened. Welshmen were always Taff, Scotsmen always Jock etc. I dare say many had kept their dislike of their nick-names to themselves but I felt it unfortunate that in hiding their true feelings they had caused another hammer to crack a nut situation and the 'Bungalows' of this world would be the nuts. Where was the common-sense view with regard to those harmless nick-names which caused no pain at all? Another 'Baby thrown out with the bath water' perhaps? My view was that this was a needless change of shape in the grand order of important things.

I also learned on this course that a dog handler tracking a suspect was asked to report his latest position and when he responded, he said, "We're just passing the 'CHINKY' Sarge". You've guessed it, he was suspended for referring to the Chinese Restaurant as the 'CHINKY'. I can't imagine that he received anything but an admonishment of some sort or other but I certainly wondered whether we were now losing the plot. God help me, I would have been sacked long ago if all these new rules and regulations had been in force when I did the job, and that was not so long ago then! It was as if the recruits were being treated as automatons and I had to again ask myself "Where was the common sense"?

So let us peep into the meaning of the word 'Diversity'.

Mr Google (or should that be Mrs. Google,) informs me that there are several meanings but in this context, it relates to the practice or quality of including or involving people from a range of different social and ethnic backgrounds and of different genders, sexual orientations etc. "Equality and Diversity should be supported for their own sake."

It is about what makes each of us unique and includes our background, personality, life experiences and beliefs, all of the things that make us who we are. It is a combination of differences that shape our views of the world, our perspective and our approach.

There are tons of explanations on the internet but basically, it is the above which organisations, such as the police were told to take account of. This diversity could be internal, external, organisational and worldview – and should aim to represent them all.

OK, I know what you are thinking: old Coppers such as myself, were bound to wonder what had gone wrong with the world. True, to a certain extent but at the same time, I firmly believe and have always believed that no-one should be hurt, whether intentionally or not, by others using any derogatory terms. To do so, is a form of bullying and should cease in all living experiences. So, I shall plead 'almost guilty' but let us now look at our fairer sex within that context.

Sex Discrimination

Sex Discrimination was made subject of legislation in 1975, twelve years after I first joined the force as a regular constable. The Equality Act 2010 with some amendments is the latest version of it.

When I joined the service in 1963 after my three years as a cadet and for a long time afterwards, the number of policewomen were few indeed. In Herefordshire, the first policewomen to be appointed were in 1947. Vera Hadley, the wife of a well-known ex 'Resident Beat' and latterly 'Scenes of Crime' officer Ted (R.I.P.) of my day, compiled a book from research carried out by her husband and a friend. The photograph below entitled, **'The first policewomen to be appointed, 1947'** was first published in the Hereford

Times newspaper and is taken from her book, 'Herefordshire Constabulary 1857 -1967. (ISBN 0-9536792-0-9)

(Photograph reproduced by courtesy of The Hereford Times).
The first Police-Women to be appointed, 1947.
Back row, L. to R: PW 6 R.E. Smith, PW 8 E.M. Watkins, PW 11 E.S. Phillips, PW 7 O.M. Hughes,
PW 9 W.A. Garrett, PW 10 P. Jones-Newton.
Front row, L. to R: PW 4 M.T. Oxton, WDC 3 J. Edwards, DCC T.B. Wheeler, Chief Constable F. Newton,
PWSergeant 1 D.B. Simpson, PW 2 K. Elias, PW 5 D. Slater.

Four of these police women were still serving in my day and I have recently made contact with two who are still alive. - PW 11 Lena Phillips and PW 4 Muriel Oxton. The PW Sergeant Simpson must have retired because the lady sat on the extreme right, Doris Slater had become the Sergeant in charge before I joined.

Some of them would enjoy portraying the macho image and could use the same men's rough language and mannerisms. Others could easily throw a drunk out of a pub and some of them could do neither. I have to admit here, that as untrue as it was, I often described **some** police women of my day as, "Having hairs on their chests"!

I can tell you that admitting that has taken some courage but come on now, everyone will hopefully understand that this was my way (among males) of very generally portraying some of the women of the force to be inclined on the macho side and as said already, no way would anyone believe that that description was true. (At least I can't confirm my comment to be true, by the way!)

In typical chauvinistic fashion, I would have said that in jest, but of course, I now know that if that comment ever should have reached the ears of our lady officers, it would have been highly offensive. In these days of course, I realise that in any event, those sorts of expressions have since been outlawed and I hasten to add, rightly so. Hands up; I should have been shot!

We had one Detective Policewoman at Worcester. (I'm not calling them 'police officers' because Policewomen was what they were then) Her name was cryptically similar to Dolly Runner and those knowing her will recognise who she was by that pseudonym. She was a rather large lady who knew every villain in Worcester as well as many of the population. The villains were as afraid of her as they were of any others of the male Detective Constables. 'Renowned' was the adjective which comes to mind.

She was a single lady as far as I knew and equal to any task performed by her males colleagues. For a pastime, she held a salmon fishing licence and often pulled one out of the River Teme.

Indeed, and generally speaking, it was a long time before many of our police ladies shook off that macho reputation, though some never deserved it in the first place. The expression I sadly used was one of those expressions which would be covered by the 'tar brush' syndrome because although I cannot recall that any were married, some were indeed, attractive and subsequently married. Indeed, I have made contact with two of these now married ex police women during my research for this book.

It wasn't until the early sixties when I recall the buzz circulating when a beauty queen, the first 'Miss ATV' (A Midlands TV Company) was recruited into our Herefordshire force. She didn't stay for very long, and although I don't know for sure, this was possibly as a result of the attention she received from her male colleagues of positive and negative stereotypes. I merely mention this because this mid-sixty period would have been when generally, more women were attracted to the force, to do the job normally done by the 'Police – Man'. They were to lose their 'Police Woman' tag just prior to the Sex Discrimination Act of 1975.

It is thanks to some of those later female officers, Jackie Bristow (now Perkins), Julie Lloyd (now Rees) and Jean Mulcaster who have taken the trouble to let me know what their early feelings were in the face of discrimination, that I'm able to include them here.

As can be seen, in the photograph, there were just eleven police women and I don't believe that in our Herefordshire days, there were many more than eleven right up until at least, the 1st October 1967 amalgamation of forces. Indeed, according to Vera Hadley's book, only ten were on the nominal role on 30th September, the eve of the amalgamation.

Who would believe, that only eight years after that amalgamation, the number of women joining the force as a whole, had exploded following the Sex Discrimination and Equal Opportunities legislation? The wave of opportunities then came their way. It was this, that opened the door to career women and which has given many female officers the opportunity to contend for the top jobs some now hold.

I hesitate here, thinking of the words which will more accurately reflect my views. This hesitation grows from the respect I hold for our female generation more than anything else. I would not have wanted either of my two daughters to have joined the police to share and witness the experiences of my own journey. I'm sure they could have coped but I would have to ask myself, "why should they"? (One did become a fingerprint expert) I would want them to be shielded from the ugly side of the job in having to deal with some of the 'scum' and circumstances that I met on my long journey.

But who am I to dictate the necessity of such protection? I am a traditionalist so my fears would not have been so strong if female officers had remained in their traditional specialist roles as experts in the field of dealing with women, children and the vulnerable in our society. However, the fact is, that if asked now, I feel sure that most would want to continue what they are now doing as equals to their male counterparts.

Supervising female police officers and viewing television programs about women in the police service has helped me redress the balance of my views. Yet I have no doubt that some, if not most , have experienced some sort of 'hurt' through being sexually discriminated against.

So far as my own experience of supervising female officers is concerned, I recall receiving a small delegation of officers and civilians of both sexes to complain that one of their number, a female police officer was always last to report for duty in the force operations room. Without going into detail, it became necessary for me to broach the subject with this officer and no sooner as I informed her of the situation, she burst into tears and ran out of the office.

My guess that she had locked herself in the ladies toilet was correct and so I briefed another civilian female support staff friend of hers to see if she could extricate the officer from the toilets. She also ended up in tears and both were locked in the toilet together. Of course, the situation eventually returned to normal, the police woman apologised and was never late again. I realise that nothing much can be taken from this experience other than the thought that maybe female officers ought to be supervised by officers of their own gender, as they had been prior to equal opportunities.

Also, in the early days when women gained the most senior of the ranks, my inward fears which weren't aired with many for fear of getting sued, was that the pressure on forces to have female officers seen as equals, probably led to some reverse discrimination. Equal opportunities had suddenly exploded and heaven help those who weren't practicing it. Whether that is true or not, as Cressida Dick and others have discovered, they have probably been more heavily targeted for criticism than their male colleagues.

I write this in the weeks prior to the first female officer being appointed as Chief Constable of my old West Mercia Force. I am satisfied that she will not have been chosen as a 'token' but I'm not so sure about those who reached such heights long before her. (I have no need to creep – I'm long retired!!)

That was my view and I refer to it now for the sake of it being how I viewed the situation then. If I did not speak my mind due to being 'Diversity' conscious that would only serve to blur the issue. I repeat that I am not at all racist or prejudiced in any shape or form other than when the 'reverse discrimination' cards are played, because I believe the playing of them is discrimination in itself.

I have friends who are senior female police officers and I know they are well worthy of the ranks they hold or have held. It should always be the best qualified person for the job without fear or favour which includes any sway caused by reverse discrimination.

So back to my story about women being part of 'The People' we employed.

My youngest daughter served many years as a fingerprint expert but in her boredom many years later, she decided to be a theatre manager. However, she married a police officer and that had nothing to do with me. He's a great son in law (and a degree holder) and retired as a Chief Superintendent in the Thames Valley Constabulary. I have never encouraged or discouraged my daughter in her employment. (Nor would she let me)

Their daughter, my granddaughter, Bella obtained a first class with honours degree in criminology and began her working life in a prison. (Much to my private concern). She is now working in London for a charity with an objective of dissuading young people from joining gangs or otherwise getting involved in criminality. Again, I fear for her and have actually thought that she might be safer in the police service. So what do I know?

So why not ask yourself the question – 'Would you encourage your own daughters or granddaughters to join the police? I'm sure that for a variety of reasons, there would be an assortment of answers. What I am sure about is that all those women now serving are doing what they want to do, in the way they want to do it and who should try to dissuade them? No-one.

I am obviously swayed by my experiences stemming from the days before equal opportunities. Policewomen earned slightly less than their male colleagues but didn't work twenty-four hour shifts and weren't expected to roll around in gutters with drunks or face the everyday threats which face them today. Pay was an issue because I believe that owing to their not paying so much National Insurance and pension contributions, this brought their pay up to almost the same as their male colleagues. There was resentment felt about that.

They were a specialist department trained to deal with children and the female gender. They would be called out as matrons to deal with female prisoners, to look after children either in trouble or being neglected, or to enquire into missing persons. They knew their counterparts in Social Services departments and did their jobs extremely well because that was what they were trained to do.

They were specialists, but even then as I have since been told by a policewoman who resigned many years ago who never worked with equal rights legislation, they often came into contact with men in the course of their duties and a point she wished to make very strongly was that not only would she prefer to work as she did as a specialist, she felt she was more respected by her male colleagues than they are today.

The lady in question helping me with my research had joined the Worcestershire Constabulary as a cadet and subsequently, as a policewoman. She married a male colleague and divulged to me that her husband did not want her to continue working on the force, so she resigned to respect his feelings.

That statement corroborated my view of how I consider we should use female police officers today. However, her view was that if the women of today were asked for their views, then most likely they would prefer to remain on equal duties, rather than being specialised.

The supposition that our female officers are more likely to receive support or 'back up' having been sent to jobs which might turn nasty, doesn't support the equality issue. The sad fact is that resources may, and often are not there, to be relied upon.

I recall two occasions when as the investigating officer, I received statements in connection with different rapes. One in 1972, prior to equal opportunities legislation and the other a few years following that legislation. (Subject of the press clipping below)

The statement from the first rape was taken by a policewoman who had received training in the taking of such statements. The statement was so good, she received a commendation for doing just that. I recall someone saying that they could actually smell the rapist just by reading the statement she had taken from the attacked young girl. It contained some good background information and intricate details of the offence and the attacker which went a long way in detecting the rapist who had an alibi which we found difficult to break.

The latter statement was also taken by a policewoman but she had never worked in the specialist 'Policewomen's Department' and had received no specialist training in that subject.

She recorded the statement purely because she was of the same gender as the victim. That made common sense; however, the statement fell well below the standard required.

It was critical that we improve the statement which led to my eventually discussing the matter with the complainant and her mother together and they had no objections at all to me recording the young girl's statement myself.

A MAN who raped a 14-year-old girl collapsed in the dock yesterday after a judge jailed him for 18 years "to cut short his career of debauchery."

Stephen Smith (43), a plant operator, of Malvern, Worcestershire, was found guilty at Shrewsbury Crown Court of raping the girl eight days after getting married.

Prosecuting conusel, Mr. John Field Evans Q.C., told the jury that in the period leading up to the rape Smith led a double life.

While living with the girl and her mother he also had an association with a woman, whom he secretly married while still seeing the girl's mother.

On the day of the rape in January he phoned the girl's mother inviting her to see a house in Worcester which the woman thought was a prospective future home.

After she left, Smith went to her home where the girl was alone, pushed her on a bed and raped her.

Smith at first told police the girl led him on. In evidence he denied having sexual contact with her.

He said he went there merely to pick up some clothing and car documents.

Det. Chief Insp. Brian Humphries said Smith had two previous convictions for rape and others for assault with intent to ravish and abduction. He was on parole when he raped the 14-year-old girl.

Mr. Justice Melford Stevenson told Smith: "You have a horrifying record, you are a grossly over-sexed man and a danger to women and young girls."

75

The offender was hell bent on denying the allegation but was an 'animal' with similar convictions who, on 9th June 1978 was eventually sentenced at Shrewsbury Crown Court to 18 years Imprisonment by the 'Hanging Judge' Lord Melford Stevenson. (Who, by the way, I shall mention again later)

And so, I have beaten about the bush for quite a while until finally, declaring my own opinion on the subject which is that whilst female officers have an important role to play within the force, they should be employed as they were prior to equality. Ladies are not equal to men when it comes to doing the same work. They are generally not built of the same stature or as strong and hence more vulnerable to harm and should be protected. They therefore cannot expect to be protected by their male counterparts.

By the same token, male officers should not generally be expected to deal with females if that can be avoided. Since equal opportunities, we are left with no specialist officers for dealing with female victims or witnesses.

If they wish to, shouldn't women always retain the qualities their gender provides and use them to good effect? Why, in various circumstances when employed by the police, shouldn't they be allowed to retain their femininity and carry out specialisms which can make them better than their male colleagues in carrying out those duties?

I can hear the howls of discontent by those who have both held their femininity and who would still rather do what the men do as a matter of course. Sure, then let them carry on and accept that notion. But why not let those who would prefer to specialise, remain so engaged This may make it easier to facilitate 'part time' working so that pregnancies and child care can be incorporated with the demands of work, and domestic lives. As opposed to the special measures which currently are provided for motherhood and career breaks.

I was also lucky enough to gain the view of a Policewoman, long retired but had the following to say about her time in the force - *"I know that today's police women would not put up with the treatment we did. I often watch the police programmes on TV and can't believe the amount of 'kit' they are issued with. All I ever had was a whistle and a bike!! Certain sergeants made life very difficult, for me in particular, I never knew the reason why, I suspect they were not very keen on female officers. Or maybe just not very nice men. I enjoyed my time but would never do it again."*

Whilst historically not many police women were assaulted by men who, despite their wrongdoing would not under any circumstances, assault a woman, increasingly there are men who have, and they don't appear to care about doing so.

Sex, Sex and More Sex

Our 'Drill Sergeant' Goff Arnold employed at the Number 8 District Police Training Centre at Bridgend, was a legend and everyone trained there during his regime will remember him. He had been a Sergeant Major in the Welsh Guards, and he suffered from that ailment called – 'Short Man's syndrome', but everyone who knew him will remember him with affection.

He'd march up and down with his pace stick under his left arm and one wondered how he could see with the peak of his cap being slashed to almost a vertical angle over his nose. Unfortunately for us from Herefordshire, that training centre took recruits from the numerous small forces in the whole of Wales plus just the one English Force – Ours of course!

With Herefordshire being famous for its white-faced cattle, to him, we had become "Those White-faced Bastards!" With our helmet plates clearly displaying 'Herefordshire Constabulary', he would walk up and down our ranks shouting in a loud piercing voice which turned his cheeks a rosy red, "Where are those White-faced Bastards"?

Where was 'Diversity' then? We were in for a torrid time for thirteen weeks facing this abuse and being singled out as anything other than 'Welsh'. I certainly didn't have the guts then to tell him that "Actually Sarge, I was born down the road at Cardiff".

If subsequently, you met someone who had also been trained at Bridgend, it wasn't long before his name was mentioned. We knew he didn't mean it really and some of the advice he gave us I remember very well. One such item concerned 'SEX'. **"Keep it in your trousers"** he would shout – **"Women, property and money will get you the sack, mark my words; shagging will get you in trouble and some of you here today will not be drawing your pension because of it!"**

He was so right and even though 'shagging' as he put it, wasn't a criminal offence, if it wasn't your wife, as a member of a police force, it could still get you into trouble. **'JOIN THE FORCE AND GET A DIVORCE'** was the motto often repeated. Having it off with someone else's wife could cause domestic disharmony in two households at the same time and that could cause trouble and trouble could cause a court appearance or a disciplinary hearing for bringing the force into disrepute. I've seen it so many times.

We were all men at Bridgend because police women were trained at a separate establishment. By heck, there would have been a few sackings for sure if that hadn't been the case!

But of course, anything but 'straight' sex was hardly mentioned. There were so many acts of sexual behaviour that were criminal offences, too many to mention here. All this sex stuff was like a jungle and if you were lucky enough to find your way through it without a fuss, you were, indeed, lucky. I should say, you were either lily white or had never been caught.

Like many others, I had not been taught about anything to do with sex; neither at home nor at school. What was there to know? Obviously we knew about the reproductive cycle of rabbits and it didn't even take us Secondary Modern Schoolboys (there were no girls,) much time to realise that rabbits weren't too different to us when it came to making babies. Seeing buckets of water being thrown over dogs having sex in the street was, I suppose, a helpful clue!

Straight or Not Straight?

But was there one dog of each sex? We (the Royal we) never thought about any alternative. I guess I was in the majority who, from early fiddling, fondling and viewing 'X' rated films when under age or reading all about

78

love and what went with it, thought that I would eventually graduate and earn my degree, if you know what I mean.

I suspect that homosexuality was the first so called 'unnatural' thing I got to learn about sex; what might be referred to as 'deviation' or 'unnatural sex'. They (those who practiced it) were referred to as 'Homos' or 'Queers'. They were obviously, or so we thought, queer because that was unnatural – again, so we thought.

We were once all stopped at the school gates by the police who told us that an incident in the school meant that we had the day off. Being turned away by the police at my school gates was something of a dream. This was especially good because other schools in Hereford had been given the day off because Princess Alexandra was visiting various establishments in Hereford and we, the boys of 'The Academy' as our school was offensively referred to, did not.

We later learned that a teacher's body had been found doubled up inside a dustbin in the boys toilets . There was no foul play involved and because of my later police cadetship, in the CID I saw the photographs and learned that he had been found in this position wearing ladies clothes and make up with half coconut shells beneath his clothes to represent breasts. Having performed some sexual gratification exercise, he had suffocated himself through his inability to extricate himself from the dustbin. What an awful way to go and how embarrassing would that be for his family. He was such a nice chap too.

Of course, during the span of my police career, I have experienced similar sudden death incidents often by hanging, when apparently being in the state of almost complete suffocation brings sexual gratification.

So, what has all this sex stuff got to do with the type of people we accept into the Police Service? I would say, it has a lot to do with it, because I have worked through times when, if such recruits were discovered to be that way inclined or sexually oriented so as not to be considered 'straight' they would not, under any circumstances, be welcomed into the police force. Many were dispensed with after appointment having been discovered to be 'Peeping Toms', knicker thieves or homosexually inclined, they all popped up from time to time. Being criminal offences was sufficient to 'kick them out' but believe you me, it was diverse sex orientation which came first on the list to those responsible for their dismissal.

The Wolfenden Committee reported in 1957, recommended the decriminalisation of private *homosexual activity between consenting adults* over the age of 21 but with heavier penalties for those who performed homosexuality in public places. It was the Sexual Offences Act of 1967 that made homosexual activity between consenting adults, legal and in 1994, the age of consent was reduced to 18.

Even as late as 1983, as a Subdivisional Commander I received a telephone call one evening informing me that one of our young police officers had been arrested at New Street Railway Station, Birmingham. He had been discovered kissing and cuddling another man in the public toilets. This was a crime, as being in a public place made it unlawful. My views on gay men were that they were weak wristed and spoke with a higher-than-normal pitch and acted in a feminine type of manner. So what was this 'he man' captain of the football team, snooker team and weight lifter, doing in the toilets with this man?

My perception, since confirmed by many a rugby player, footballer or other athlete coming out of their closets, had been completely wrong and misplaced. Such sexual inclinations by both sexes exist across the whole spectrum of society.

I managed to persuade the powers that be in the Transport Police that the best way to deal with our PC was to hand him over to me to let 'The Force' deal with it. It was, of course, a serious breach of Police Regulations to discredit the force, not to speak of the criminal offence. He was later given police bail to appear at a police station on another day.

This wasn't by far, the most pleasant of experiences for me. I telephoned the Deputy Chief Constable, the Chief Officer with the 'Discipline' portfolio of the force. "What do you want me to do with him Sir"? Was my plea. There were only two options – Charge him or get his ticket, (the vernacular for resignation) and let sleeping dogs lie. The latter was the only option I was given.

Following my initial discussions with the officer, I learned that he wasn't disposed to resign. I had already had the unfortunate job of letting his mother know of the circumstances of his arrest by telephone prior to leaving for New Street Railway Station. Now, I had the awful task of driving him to Hereford to hand him over to his parents. This wasn't the best of receptions I had experienced in my service. I had hoped that his parents could see the sense in what I was trying to do and so I decided to leave them to discuss it having arranged to meet his mother at our police station during the following day.

An accompanying colleague and I went straight back to Bromsgrove where, from inside his single men's accommodation, we recovered numerous letters and cards from other men which plainly corroborated the surprising revelation concerning this 'macho' man's private life. These documents etc. were, of course, treated as exhibits, because we were still dealing with what was a crime and this was circumstantial and corroborating evidence, just in case he was to come up with a story about helping a man in distress or similar.

Finally, the constable decided to resign. This was a sad situation because he had been a young officer with potential and may well have progressed in the service had he kept his private life within the confines of the law.

The circumstances become even melancholier because these days he could openly be gay and as such welcomed into the police service and invited to join the 'Lesbian and Gay Police Association' which was founded only seven years following this incident. The association represents the needs and interests of gay and bisexual police officers and police staff in the United Kingdom. Members can be found in all UK Police Forces.

[The Association changed its name to Gay Police Association (GPA) following a vote of its membership in 2001.]

Open homosexuality is something that society has predominantly learned to embrace, there is a greater understanding of all the issues and it has lost the stigma previously attached to it. No-one should be able to use their knowledge of an individual's sexual preference to gain advantage, and decriminalisation has been an important element in that process and one that allows members of the community to consider the police.

I feel that previously, apart from the legality issue, there was a fear that non-police people becoming aware of such leanings, or sexual orientations, could place those officers under heavy strain of being 'beholden' and therefore open to blackmail or coercion. Other professional people such as politicians, vicars, doctors have previously been subjected to such threats. So was this change a good thing or a bad thing?

Acting as the constable did in public toilets is still a criminal offence but, of course, had he come out of the closet then, as he might well have done now, there would be no need to commit such criminal acts at all. We obviously live during different times and all this just adds weight to the police service being made up as a microcosm of society. That, in itself, is a 'Good Thing.' Since those days have now changed, when coming out of the closet is the normal practice, those strains have now all disappeared. I am therefore left with the notion that it is a good thing but should not be flaunted by those concerned.

Race, Creed or Colour

My school-day views of the late 1950s about people of a different race, creed or colour, were probably the same as most others. In fact, those people with different coloured skins or who spoke with a foreign accent, were few and far between in Herefordshire. Most were classed as 'British White'.

I can't remember when I became aware that people were becoming cautious and probably suspicious about the growing population of those who were different. They weren't from around here, spoke a different language and if they spoke our language, it was with a peculiar accent which made them difficult to understand. I didn't know it then, but they also had different religions and places of worship.

I was of course, to learn that they were from a variety of different backgrounds from that *'great big melting pot, big enough to take the world and all its got'*. (As recorded by 'Blue Mink' in 1969). They represented a broad spectrum of educational standards and professions; indeed, some were here from comparatively poor countries but came to help us continue to make our country even richer than theirs in more ways than one.

Some simply viewed our home countries as being paved with gold and represented huge opportunities for them. In many cases it was only the men who came and who, from their meagre wages, saved sufficiently to enable their families to join them.

So, from that simple 'backcloth' it seems quite easy to me to understand how prejudices grew. My view was that this latter group of people in particular, were regarded as cheap labour and as such, with their strange cultures, automatically created a lower spectrum of status than our own. As they were already on the bottom rung of our ladder, they automatically promoted those white people who were previously on that rung, to a higher status. Subconsciously, those promoted would naturally want to keep the new arrivals firmly in place at the bottom of the pile.

Then, of course, when these aliens (yes, I know what they are now) began to make good for themselves, wasn't it natural for the 'promoted' white to feel threatened by their successes? Our government had helped them settle and obtain accommodation and employment. Why should they enjoy the same levels of support and recognition as our home grown?

This view may have been held by a silent proportion of our society but inevitably, there would be some who would shout it aloud from the rafters even without knowing the true reasons for their emigration.

When as a Hereford United 'Ball Boy I helped to build the standing terraces behind the Merton Meadow goal. We had tons of earth to move with hand shovels and wheelbarrows. I suspect earth moving machines were too expensive for our small club to hire.

 A Military camp had been built at Foxley, near Mansell Lacy located about nine miles from Hereford and in the early years of the last war, personnel arrived there; first came the Canadians, then the Americans and after the war the camp housed Polish refugees unable to return home. Later, many found temporary shelter in these former army huts due to the post-war housing shortage.

It was these many 'Poles' Ooops Polish and I believe some refugees from the Hungarian Revolution who were transported to Edgar Street to help shovel this mountain of earth. They had language difficulties, but of course, they were white, so that helped them evade some of the prejudices and though a very long time ago, I cannot recall them being treated any differently than ourselves.

So far as black people were concerned, I cannot ever remember in those days, being aware of any black families living in Hereford. Being a football supporter, I know that one of the first black players to play in our English leagues was Tommy Best who was my hero for many years because he played for Hereford United and as a centre forward, scored many, if not most of our goals. When still at Primary School, I used to stand between my dad's legs watching the team and even though Tommy finished his career in 1955 when I was only eleven, I can remember him well from those 66 years ago.

The following is a short extract of a larger article taken from the Hereford Times dated 17th September 2018: -

THE first black footballer to play for Hereford United died yesterday, aged 97.
Tommy Best helped to break down many racial barriers with his goalscoring exploits when non-white footballers were a rarity. He

played for Chester, Cardiff City and Queens Park Rangers before finishing his career at Edgar Street..

In total, he made 145 appearances for the Bulls between 1950 and 1955, scoring 67 goals. Mr Best remained in Hereford on retiring and lived in Whitecross where he and wife Eunice had three children, Jennifer, Paul and Judy. Jennifer said they all agreed that he was a brilliant dad.

Born in Milford Haven to a father from Barbados, there was a great support among football fans for Best to represent Wales. He was told by the management team at Cardiff City that he would represent his country when Trevor Ford was injured but, much to his disappointment, the call did not come.

Speaking to the Western Daily Press in 1998, Mr Best said he could only assume the omission was down to the colour of his skin.

"You have to remember that black players were a rarity then. And I'm forced to the conclusion that I was a victim of prejudice," he told the paper.

"I simply know I deserved to play for Wales."

However, Mr Best never talked about racism with his children – and also explained in the newspaper interview in 1998 that a footballer's job is to "concentrate on the ball and shut his ears to what the spectators may be saying"..................

Of course, he would have been unable to shut his ears to what the spectators may have been shouting at him. I never heard racist comments but I suspect he suffered them probably more so in those days than now.

It seems natural therefore, that they were treated differently with suspicion and disdain. But times have marched on and I believe it is a tragedy that the government has had to introduce a raft of legislation in an effort to force us to act without prejudice against these people and their ambitions.

Surely laws cannot do that? They merely suppress voices or actions which demonstrate racial tension. But whilst laws can't directly dictate a curb on racism within those who hold these views, they must help because if such voices are silenced and actions not seen, then that will have a positive consequence in not encouraging others to demonstrate or may even curb their thoughts.

So, as much as I can understand those very early prejudices, I can see no reason whatsoever why these so called 'foreigners', who are now, by the way, British citizens of second, third and fourth generations should be prejudiced in any way from joining our police forces or any other vocation, or to be embodied into our society as being equal to anyone else.

These minority peoples have now received the same levels of education as their fellow neighbours who are native to their countries of origin. For many years now, the children of our original immigrants have managed to reach the highest levels of what is now their society in all spheres of academia, professional employment, sports and pastimes. The only remaining differences visible are their skin colour and sometimes the accents handed down by previous generations.

How sad it was, to have to insert here, this paragraph which followed the England football team losing on a penalty 'shoot out' to Italy in the 2021 European Football championships. It so happened that the three penalties missed by English players were taken by black players. An avalanche of racist comment, mostly contained in social media followed. These individuals were classed as morons and where it has been possible to identify them, some of their local clubs have justifiably banned them for life for entering their stadia. It just goes to show that prejudice cannot be ironed out by laws.

It had taken a long time to get to where we are and whilst I'm sure that prejudices in some will continue to linger, I was delighted to have a conversation with my grandson who recently left his secondary school to move to a Sixth Form college. He sent me photographs of his classmates all celebrating their leaving school and, of course, some were black and so I intentionally raised the subject of colour in our subsequent conversation.

Maybe I shouldn't have as I could see from the expressions on his face that he wondered why I had bothered. He could see no differences at all in his mates, whether black or white and he went out of his way to enforce that view. "Good for him" I thought.

However, I have copied these words again from that written a little earlier:-

> *So, as much as I can understand those very early prejudices, I can see no reason whatsoever why these so called 'foreigners', who are now, by the way, British citizens of second, third and fourth generations should be prejudiced in any way from joining our police forces or any other vocation, or to be embodied into our society as* **being equal** *to anyone else.*

For an obvious reason, I have placed the words 'being equal' in enlarged bolden text because I believe in our efforts to make this equality happen, we have possibly created problems for ourselves in applying reverse discrimination by allowing the unequal talents of black and other immigrant races, to be placed in positions of power and influence over others who may be better qualified than them. I really believe that if a black man or woman is the best candidate, then he / she should be treated as such and given the job.

On the other hand, if the weaker black person (or woman in the context of sex discrimination) is pushed ahead of better candidates because of their sex, colour or creed, then my belief is, that this will do nothing but harm to the cause of equality. Resentment will surely be experienced by those affected and to be frank, who can blame them?

I worked for many months in Bermuda and had a great deal to do with the Commissioner, Jean-Jaques LeMay, a secondee from the Royal Canadian Mounted Police (RCMP) and his deputy George Jackson who, though originally from St Vincent and the Grenadines, was black and for all intents and purposes, was the local man. I had initially been introduced to this top tier management of the force by the head of the fingerprint bureau, Detective Inspector Howard Cutts who transferred there from the Metropolitan Police.

The Islands of Bermuda are British Overseas Territories but whilst the British Government keeps almost an unseen eye on Bermuda, the government of

Bermuda is largely self-governing. I got to know many of the government ministers and my impression was that whilst they had placed a heavy reliance on aid from Canada, England and the USA, to lead the way in various vocations, education and training, they were now at a stage when people such as Commissioner Jean-Jaques LeMay, could release the reins and hand over to local people.

The Commissioner was a member of the Association of Caribbean Commissioners of Police. (ACCP) With Cayman and the Bahamas, they were countries far more advanced than other Caribbean countries I had worked in and that was just about all of the main inhabited ones whose commissioners were members of the ACCP.

It was whilst I worked in Bermuda that Jean-Jaques was to end his secondment and just about all I had spoken to were expecting the black George Jackson to take over from him. Indeed, it was a locally born man that became commissioner, the only problem being that it wasn't George, it was a white man Jonathan Smith. Someone who I had not previously met.

The force had quite a good 'standalone' computer fingerprint searching system but it didn't take long to persuade them, with other Caribbean countries, to have access to our vast England and Wales database. All that had to be done was for the ministers and the Commissioner to give it the thumbs up so that they could join our consortium.

The new Commissioner, had that week, just taken over the chair. He persuaded the ministers that because he had not had the time to fully understand the system, that he would rather the decision be delayed until he had. This was an Interpol concept, and our team couldn't believe it as we had invested a huge amount of money in getting them on board. He sat on the fence for such a long time, that they never did 'get on board' before the system was eventually taken over by the second-generation system in 2001.

The following has been taken from a publication which I believe stems from the rank and file of the Bermudian Police called Police.com. It was very critical of Jonathan Smith and one wonders whether the black editorial team were biased in any way. The headline read: -

A useful contribution to the Bermuda Police service or a politically correct PR opportunist?

Chief Cop but what's he in it for? A fence sitter without imagination, enthusiasm or initiative? Who knows, nothing appears to have changed under this leader and my first-hand dealings with him cause me to question whether he's a 'yes' man with little interest in anything other than getting to the top for reasons other than ensuring policing is undertaken and the community provided a service. See the remarks about the investigation and complaint (below). Also watch the news - nothing appears to have changed in 10+ years.

John 'Boy' Smith appears to accept what this site has advised for years: "BERMUDA HAS A PROLIFIC DRUG TRADE" The island's youngest commissioner with a questionable investigative ability? Does he have a clue what goes on within his own police force or is he kept from it by his deputy and assistant (below)? Read 'Morale'.

As with every police Bermudian officer, one questions why, if they are competent individuals, they do not get a real job, a professional position and salary to match. With regard to Jonathan, the youngest commissioner of police Bermuda has ever seen, to give him some credit, it appears he saw an opportunity; a lack of skill in the service and that it would take little to rise to the surface ...

Inspector Smith replaced Jean-Jacques LeMay as commissioner of police in April 2000. Very strange when one considers that only four years earlier there were concerns expressed about the Bermudian officers lack of overseas training and very little training occurred subsequent to 1997. A Bermuda Sun article in 1997 advised:

The above paragraphs have been taken from a much larger item in that publication but I publish it here, as merely an example of how discrimination

89

was exercised in those days. It was said by most that the black George Jackson who, although a very pleasant chap, in no way matched the skills and professionalism of Jean-Jaques LeMay.

I have not kept watch or caught up with events in Bermuda since but having searched for the current management team, I find that Stephen Mark Corbishley was appointed Commissioner in August 2018. He was born in Manchester and graduated from Christ Church University, Canterbury. He attended the 2016 Strategic Command Course and transferred to Bermuda from the Kent County Constabulary. Mr Corbishley's deputy is a black man as is one of his two Assistant Commissioners.

In fairness to the situation, it appears that the Island is so small that although high profile banking crimes abound, apart from the drugs trade and the odd homicide, the experience required of a commissioner, cannot be found on the Island. That is a doubtful generous guess, but these people are appointed by a black government and one wonders why they don't second their own to Canadian, or UK forces to reap that experience.

Returning to our home lands, another factor which I believe has not helped in causing a quicker resolution and more peaceful harmony to this difficult subject, is the fact that because our immigrants were suffering early prejudices, they were virtually forced to build enclaves which became ghettos. This, of course was the cause of those prejudices but coupled with a desire to feel safer in 'keeping together'. Hindsight suggests that it would have helped tremendously if they had been more effectively integrated into their new societies.

Thankfully, those other than the first-generation immigrants now speak good English but who can blame them for wanting to retain the traditions from where they came, especially when they were raised by their previous generation? This is a difficult subject but I'm *almost sure* that if, as a young man, I went to live permanently in say, India, then I would do all I could to melt into their country and adopt their culture where I could.

Another small issue I have is in regard to what people of a colour other than 'white' are referred to. The 'N' word was often used as was the term, 'Half Cast', being from mixed parenthood. The very sound of the 'N' word and the way it was used, conveys a derogatory tone. However, the term 'Half Cast' I personally thought was not so disparaging. It is, or was so easy to become offensive without even knowing it.

I distinctly remember attending a police race relations course when we were told that the term, 'Coloured' was regarded at the favoured adjective to describe non-white people. Yet on a course several years later, I was instructed that 'coloured' was regarded as objectionable and the adjective, 'Black' was the favoured expression.

Who is it that stipulates such things because I often have to hold myself back when about to use, what I believe to be the more favoured term of 'coloured'? I feel sure that people of almost white colour, would probably be offended when called 'Black' because black, they are not.

So, to end this conundrum, I'm certainly not racist and welcome non-white people of any colour or of course, white people from other countries into the police service. I wish other people were not racist but whatever, every job both in recruitment to the police and any other occupation should open its doors to the best candidates of whatever race, creed or colour.

Reverse discrimination is a discrimination on ordinary white people who seek the same job, however, I'm pleased that not only has the shape of our policing changed, so has the colour and may it continue.

Stop and Search et al

There is no doubt that Stephen Lawrence's murder and many similar incidents widely reported have brought shame on our vocation and the tar brush has almost worn away with over use. However, where are the exclamations of objections by our senior officers when, on many occasions, the issue of stop and search is raised?

I cannot iron out the fact that, as far as I know, and I don't claim to know, that some of such stops were caused out of a racial motivation. But come on! Where are the shouts of protest concerning the fact that in many areas, it is black people who have committed most of the types of acts the police are wishing to stop? There are also many areas where it would be difficult to find people other than with black skins.

I'm not advocating 'willy nilly' blanket searching of every black person in a particular area but it has also been fashionable for some black races to commit some types of crime, more so than white people. Among recent examples have been child prostitution, white and black slave trafficking and others all of which seem these days, to involve the funding of the drugs that they have also been known to be involved in.

Of course, this does not mean that white people do not commit such crimes and also, many innocent black people will have been caught in this net as it is not only black people who commit these offences. Any copper worth his salt will ensure that where it appears appropriate stop searches will involve white people. That is the art of policing but where there is a preponderance that they are, then I firmly believe that the tactic of stopping and searching black people in some of the crime ridden areas where they live and operate, is excellent policing. I can't recall anyone resounding : –

"But most of the crime in this area is committed by these 'Black People".

Yet, among frequent shouts of police racism, despite cases where colour has been the only reason, other observations made, such as being in possession of expensive cars and jewellery etc., especially when such persons are showing affluence when not in permanent work or even when receiving benefits, are reasons in my book, which will trigger suspicions. In my day, arrests under such circumstances would indicate that the copper had a good nose for a 'wrong one'. I find it sad that such skill has suffered through the fear of being sued or even just 'taken to task'.

It is sad that in the absence of such pleas in defence of the tactics from our senior officers, the officers now daring to make a stop and search are required to provide those stopped, with a ticket containing the below information concerning their experience: -

- **why you've been stopped and searched**

- **why they chose you**

- **what they're looking for**

- **their name and the station where they're based (unless the search is in relation to suspected terrorist activity or giving his or her name may place the officer in danger. They must then give their warrant ID number)**

- **the law under which you've been stopped**

- **your right to a copy of the form**

I cannot think of anything that would dissuade me more from stopping and searching people, but I suppose that's the objective behind the pressure to resist them. Policing is sometimes an art. One senses that a person from whatever ethnicity, is up to no good. What time of day or night is it? Where is this stop taking place? How many people are involved and what is the background crime situation in that area? These are some factors which, together with a sixth sense, makes the 'nose twitch'.

The sad part about officers holding back on stop and searches, is that they will not get to detect any crime, or indeed, gain any other intelligence, by just passing by people who, perhaps if they were not hindered by such red tape, may have ended up being arrested.

The terms 'targeted' and 'intelligence-led' are the blanket descriptions behind stop and search these days. Sadly, the intelligence-led part of that phrase is lacking because the police are likely not to be so industrious with talking to people and ferreting out information as they were before such restraints on them were applied. I wouldn't be surprised if the degree of patrols in those areas also declined for that reason. The ancient Japanese proverb "see no evil, hear no evil, speak no evil" comes to mind. "Follow your nose" was the advice given to many a copper in my younger days. This sixth sense is something that most acquired and cannot be taught or described very well. But it needs practising and that won't happen so often these days.

I recall the era just after we had been issued with Panda Cars. They were regarded as great then but they almost totally took us off the streets and involvement with the community.

The 'City' part of Hereford was dissected by the main arterial A49 Road which, so far as Herefordshire was concerned, ran from Ross on Wye, through Hereford and on towards Leominster and further north. My mate, PC 148 Tony Breeze drove Unit 1 and PC 131 Brian Humphreys, (myself) drove Unit 2. The A49 was the boundaries of our patrol areas and so, at around 2-3am on nights when we could, we'd meet up and park in a layby very near the northern end of the city where most vehicles leaving the city or entering it from the north would need to pass.

We would operate road checks of our own volition by forming a system whereby one of us would stop the car and speak to the driver. The object was to determine exactly who they were, who owned the car and what they were doing out in the middle of the night. It must be remembered that although we had radios, we did not have any form of police computer and if we wanted to know details of ownership of vehicles then this could only be obtained by calling out a 'Local Taxation Officer' who would need to return to his office and look up the records.

Leaping ahead here, in 1974 I was employed as an Operations Room Duty Inspector and was fortunate to attend one of the first Police National Computer courses being run at Hendon, the Metropolitan Police's Training School. The benefits that this brought concerning vehicle ownership, stolen vehicles, firearms records and later many other 'add on' applications are immeasurable when compared with the 'dark ages' before those times. What a beneficial change of shape that was. Our main tool then was the gift of the gab.

Tony and I caught so many drivers who had been or were about to be up to no good we were often jealously referred to by others as 'Jammy'. Not so, we had earned our luck.

The Road Safety Act 1967 also brought with it the introduction of the first Breathalyser. This was in October of that year, just a short time after the introduction of Panda cars. So now, in addition to our two-piece radios swishing about on dashboards, we had a green plastic box containing blow up bags and glass vials containing some crystals.

Unlike modern day breathalysers, the idea was that the ends of the glass vials were sawn off by inserting them into a slot on the side of the container and sawing them backwards and forwards until the ends snapped off. The bag was then inserted onto one end of the vial and the suspect would blow into the other end. Following this, the crystals at the end of the vial were examined and if they turned green above a certain line, then this indicated alcohol levels were above the limit and the suspect could be arrested for further tests at the police station.

It is ironic that whilst the Police National Computer (PNC) and Automatic Number Plate Recognition (ANPR) devices are now so good at rapidly accessing vital information, they now negate much of the communication skills we acquired by the skilful questioning of the occupants. All vehicles were stopped, whether suspected of being up to no good or otherwise; our only justification was that every honest man was now in bed at that time of the night and what were these people doing driving in, out or through our city? Such actions would now put us in jeopardy of being disciplined.

Whilst the 'chat' was going on, the other officer would slowly walk around the car. When did the tax expire and most important, where was it issued? We would examine the rubber stamp on the tax disc which told us this. (Tax discs were withdrawn in 2015.) Then we would check the lights, tyres and general condition, spotting what there was on the empty seats. If the driver was accompanied, we would or might also check out the other occupants.

If we weren't completely satisfied, then we would ask the driver to open up the boot.

The description of our above method reminds me of the joke about a similar stop when the checking officer noted that a rear light was not working. He advised the driver who apologised and told him that he would get it fixed as he had been aware of it but in the meantime, it just needed a kick and it would come on. The officer kicked it and indeed it came on. The officer then said to the driver, **"Well, you'd better kick your windscreen because your tax disc is out of date"**!

Sadly, these restraining practices have been introduced because what might have been the over exuberance, possibly racially motivated by some in larger forces where such resistance by those having something to hide, have been more vociferously heard for obvious reasons.

As an aside, it was my mate Tony Breeze, who was about to be married and so I arranged for him to take over our flat when we moved to a police house. It was common practice in those days for a collection to be organised among the shift so that we could buy our colleagues a wedding present. I distinctly remember that we bought Tony a tin bread bin. The latest fashion in bread bins was that it had to have a roll down front opening. In effect, you lifted up the front which rolled into the inside of the bin. Thinking back, it was a pretty crass present.

Whether by design or accident, Tony's marriage was to take place when he should have been on night duty. If it was planned, it wouldn't have gone down well with our supervisors because it was an unwritten rule that we would never take leave on nights. Whether this had anything to do with it, I can't recall but I hatched a plan whereby I would get Tony out of bed and get him into the police station at about 3am in the morning on some pretence purely so that we could present his wedding gift to him. He was to receive our wedding present, so how could he complain?

96

I went to the flat and rang the bell. He eventually came downstairs bog eyed and opened the door. I apologised profusely and told him that a suspect, Pat Barwick (not his real name but similar,) had assaulted and raped a woman on Castle Green and we were organising a search for him.

He dressed and doing his shoe laces up in the car, we raced off to the Station. As we walked into the parade room, he faced the entire shift. How we managed that I can't recall except that one of our Sergeants, Vic Barnes was comparatively easier to persuade. We were all there to present him with his wedding gift. This nicely examples the camaraderie we enjoyed on shift in those days though I doubt whether Tony appreciated it as much on that occasion. I took him back home in good spirits.

So in conclusion, so far as racial prejudice exists in the police force, we have come a long way to eradicate the problems but we are in a marathon still and not a sprint. But we are certainly not 'Rotten to the Core'.

7.

APPEARANCE, TRAINING AND DISCIPLINE

I have already mentioned the 'National Service' effect which contributed to the degree of discipline and conduct by those who had experienced it in the so-called, 'good old days'. We may have thought those were harsh days, particularly when we were on the wrong end of the stick: however, on reflection, I'm convinced that it benefitted us in so many ways.

Being late on parade, not submitting enough work, being off your beat, not having your uniform pressed and boots polished, not looking after your appearance generally and not keeping your notebook up to date. There were a thousand and one things that could get you on the wrong side of our supervisors. Whilst many of them would be classed as 'petty' these days, it had the effect of keeping us sharp, doing our jobs well and appearing smart which in total, I believed helped the public have confidence in us and hence respect.

I was once cheeky enough to enter the Police Station a minute or two prior to the end of my night shift. The sergeant looked at me, looked at his watch, frowned and told me to go and patrol Gaol Street, which was the address of the Station and to report for booking off duty when my shift ended. In the fear that he would be looking out of the door to check on me, I walked to the end of the Street and back again.

As petty as that was and as it might now appear, I feel sure that the absence of such discipline these days is perhaps one of many reasons why the police are appearing not to be providing the service expected by the public and have lost some of the respect they once commanded. We have become 'mamby pamby' or should I say, 'Ill-disciplined and spoilt'. I also believe the same could be said for the parent / child relationship today.

Those sergeants, or most of them, had been in the military and discipline and disciplining others came easily to them. Police absence from the streets and with it the necessity to talk to people must surely have contributed to the erosion of 'Police / Public' relationships and the confidence the public had in us. Discipline, or rather the lack of it was indeed, one of those bricks that tumbled from the wall and I was able to witness it when completing my tasks as one of the 'Retained Experienced Personnel (REP).

Fortunately for me, returning to West Mercia Constabulary twelve years after my warrant card holding retirement , allowed me to take a peek into such issues. This commenced in 2002 and finished in 2006 The new breed of sergeants had arrived and of course, a little back in the day, I was one of them. The difference however, was that I was trained by these 'old soldiers' and when I came to analyse crime reports and enquiries whilst in that 'Retained Experienced Personnel' role , (REP) my eyes were opened to sadly it must be said, 'The Blind leading the Blind'. This was confirmed by other of my later REP colleagues, some of who were required to retake the poor witness statements taken by their then, present-day colleagues.

I couldn't believe the level of incompetence I was now witnessing. Competence had dropped by all proportions and that was why the DCI of the day at Worcester called on me to examine the crimes reported and the ensuing enquiries made into them. Martin Lakeman had been a bright young officer, coincidentally under my command in my day. He had come to realise that something was wrong with the level of experience of the young officers now under his command. He was correct.

I could wander completely off the track here by giving numerous examples, but I must discipline myself in sticking to my script about the next generation who now form the police force family. In any event, placing blame on them would be wrong because in reality, it is the system of instruction, I consider to be at the root of the problem.

I realised that having policed by 'walking the beat' and then being converted to 'Unit Beat Policing' performed mostly in 'Panda' cars, I was fortunate to have received the experiences of both methods and the numerous changes which resulted. I have to say that although the shape of policing had completely changed for us at that time, it was fantastic for us riding around in these cars out of all winds and weather. In retrospect, the effect on policing in general and on police / public relationships was at the hub of change and this was mostly very negative and from which, there was no turning back.

This new generation of police officers, are young men and women doubtlessly better educated than most of us. They have experienced a different method of training and are supervised by youngsters, not much older or wiser than themselves who in the main, have not experienced such a level of discipline as was 'dished out' in previous days.

My REP scheme involvement taught me that it was now not necessary to learn parrot fashion the definitions of various crimes traffic and general police duty law. They are replaced by symposiums or 'workshops' held with the students sitting in a circle to discuss various scenarios of these so that each element of them can be discussed. There would have been merits in dropping the 'chalk and talk' methods of teaching but when mentoring this new breed of probationary constables, it became clear that they were then unfamiliar with the various elements of the crimes they were investigating.

My view was that such role-playing exercises would be fine at the time of tuition but I question whether they could have retained that information long enough to have been useful when carrying out their duties in the years after their training.

This subject of learning crime definitions is invariably raised in discussions with colleagues years after retirement. All will brag that they can recite many of them now. After 'lights out' in dormitories, some would continue learning them by use of a torch beneath the sheets before going to sleep. (Or at least that's what they said they were doing!)

If there was an advantage of being a police cadet, that was it, because we had learned our definitions long before even walking through the gates of the police training centre.

As pointless as it appeared to us at the time, we are now in unison in the belief that learning these definitions, parrot fashion, was a rapid way of determining whether a particular crime had been committed or not and hence, if the culprit was present, whether they could be arrested – or not!

However, if there is a defence for these modern-day methods, any officer unsure of the rationale for arrest, can now quickly be in communication with others for advice. Whereas in my day, officers were on their own and any question as to whether or not a person could be arrested, could not be debated until you arrived at the police station with the culprit/s.

I was fortunate enough also to be completely computer literate before most of these young officers, because, as may be recalled from my table of experience charted earlier, my first job following retirement was to join the 'Automatic Fingerprint Recognition Consortium' which involved rolling out the first computerised fingerprint storage and searching system in England and Wales.

It was necessary to use personal computers to receive and dispatch the work we were involved in. This was the foremost reason why I had been asked to log into what was then, the force's 'CRIMES' system which held the state of each crime being enquired into by the investigating officer. In short, I was more computer literate than the officers now being trained to use them in their every-day duties.

As a by-product of this work, most other Divisions were later calling for my services because a lot of what I discovered, resulted in numerous crimes being de-classified into 'No Crimes' because they weren't crimes at all. That also caused the particular detection rates to increase. On occasions, it also resulted in many crimes being detected.

The other 'by-product' of my discoveries was that as I was able to sit beside some of the probationary constables and go through the system with them;

a mentoring scheme commenced and I was joined by a few officers who had gone through the mill of similar experiences. We became united in our disappointment of supervising officers and the level of knowledge of the law they, and the bobbies under their supervision, commanded.

I can vividly recall accompanying a young policewoman who had been given a crime involving the theft of money from a patient hospitalised in the City's Royal Infirmary. She hadn't a clue where to start and had not even visited the hospital.

Although in the end, we were fairly sure who the culprit nurse was, we could never prove her guilt without a confession which was not to be forthcoming. As would be expected, we made enquiries of the nursing supervisors and other staff, who were obviously not involved in the offence, as to what their thoughts and suspicions were. The officer hadn't realised that being under investigation by the police, would often bring out inner and confidential thoughts of people held about others.

However, whilst the crime remained undetected, the whole exercise was rewarding for us both and I hoped, would have instilled in her the confidence, which she sadly lacked.

The real pleasure was the thanks I received from the officer herself. She was out of her comfort zone and this should have been picked up by her supervisors who possibly required similar guidance. Clearly she would have been frightened to death of such procedures in dealing with people on these enquiries. I left her in the knowledge that this was not so much a mysterious world after all, and also, the enquiries we made gave her the confidence to submit her file in the knowledge that all avenues of enquiry had now been exhausted.

I do not want to give the impression that I was the 'Be and End All' of policing methods. I most certainly was not, but I had fortunately been involved in and had knowledge of both methods of policing and training. This must have been almost a unique experience, and it was quite easy to identify that the comparatively young supervisors of today did not possess the skills of their colleagues of yesterday.

However, being possibly the first 'five-year' sergeant in my force with many following me, I have to say, that supervisory skills have deteriorated. The system does not appear to ensure that those promoted possess not only all the knowledge to do the job properly, but that their management and supervisory skills are honed sufficiently enough to make them good supervisors. To repeat, in so far as the people joining the job are concerned, no criticism is levelled, indeed, the opposite.

Of course, today's police personnel are far more educationally qualified than in my day and computing wasn't a tool in our armoury. However, what seemed to have been lacking was the everyday skills required to do the job which some, I guess like myself, with a shade of envy in their reasoning, may say, could have been acquired in the 'University of Life'.

Height Restrictions

I would be quite wealthy these days, if I had received a pound for every time, friends and acquaintances have commented to me about how 'dwarf like' today's officers appear when compared with their brothers and sisters of yesteryear. In so far as 'diversity' is concerned, I have to admit that I paused in the use of 'dwarf-like'. Why should I? I asked myself. This is an unfortunate condition suffered by some who are quite happy and recognise that by a quirk of their genes, makes them somewhat different in size to others.

Should the appearance of recruits matter, be they tall or short? I must be careful not to be biased about this change we've encountered. The fact of the matter is, though I'm now 6' 2½" and a bit and at 77 years of age, I just can't help noticing how police officers have suddenly appeared to have had some of their legs cut off.

The photograph on the next page is not of the best quality but I was exceedingly proud to have been selected as the cadet in this recruitment campaign. The male constable displayed is PC 29 Gabriel Quan (Gabby) who

I thought had emigrated to Australia shortly after the recruitment campaign. The advertisement indicates that constables should be 19 to 30 years, 5' 10" tall, medically fit and of good character and education.

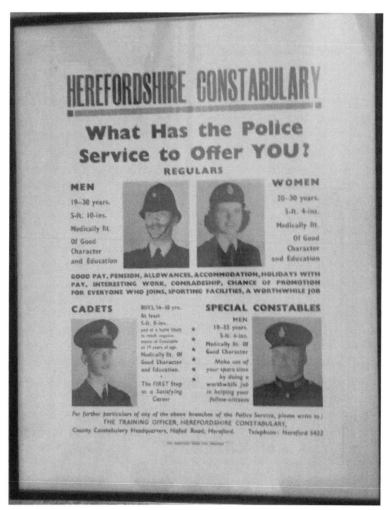

Readers, please forgive me but being interested in people and genealogy being my hobby, I couldn't resist looking him up on my genealogical databases to see if he was still alive. He might not have remembered me but I recall him very well. He was a tall, upright constable of fine bearing. I recall his nose was flattened and looked like he had been in the ring with a heavyweight boxer but he was a fine example of the smart looking constable of the day.

Sadly I was to learn that he died in Kerikeri, North Island, New Zealand on 8th June 2014. He was 79. I have since been in touch with his family who continue to reside in that same area where Gabby had earlier died.

I have been unable to trace Mary Bodenham, the policewoman in the advertisement who depicted the fact that we required 'Women' 20 to 30 years, 5' 4" tall, medically fit and of good character and education.

So, with myself representing the requirements of cadets, I know the photograph was taken before my 19th Birthday and so would have been years before equal opportunities were introduced by legislation in 1975.

I make this observation because I'm aware that at least in Herefordshire, in addition to their specialist work, although they never worked 24-hour shifts, policewomen carried out beat work until midnight, when they would have worked a 4pm to midnight shift. They regularly paraded with their shifts to be posted to beats unless they were dealing with one of their specialist duties with women or children.

I am indebted to PW Julie Lloyd (later Sergeant Julie Rees) and PW Jackie Bristow (now Jackie Perkins) who I worked with at Hereford who confirm the above practices. As an aside, I recall marching out onto our beats shortly after 10pm with Julie Lloyd and because we must have been posted to neighbouring beats, we were walking through the High Town on our way to our respective beats and walking towards us but swaying from side to side, was a man who had obviously had too much cider to drink. He wasn't disorderly or incapable and as we passed I wished him a good night. He doffed his cap and responded, "Yes, have a good night officer"........and after a slight pause he added... "And your wife"!

Julie reminded me that she often worked the beats on the south side of the river from the police station known as, you've guessed it, 'South Wye.' Not only did she deal with women and children, she policed the same areas and was directed to the same incidents as was the male beat officers who worked there.

So, the question must be asked, "As a female officer working under almost identical conditions, how could you get into the police force at 5' 4" when, as a man of 5' 9", you were classed as being too short and would be rejected? It didn't make sense.

Well, of course, I realise that with gender differences, not too many women of 5'10" would be found to recruit. Maybe allowances should have been made but how unfair is it, that those men of less than 5'10" were rejected?

This situation reminds me of one of the many occasions when I shot myself in the foot when, as a Chief Superintendent carrying out my HMI's Staff Officer duties. I happened to comment to my boss, John Woodcock (later Sir John) that the police generally looked far shorter, a factor which probably contributed to them not receiving as much respect as they did in the days when we were much taller.

His reaction was, I imagine, something that felt like stepping onto a land mine, because it had completely escaped my mind that John Woodcock was far from 5' 10"! Indeed, he was quite short but with his commanding presence and scrambled egg all over his shoulders and cap, there couldn't have been many who didn't look as smart or with such a commanding presence as himself.

He replied to me something along the lines of *"didn't you know that I was a party to the amendments made to those recruit entry requirements"?* I had walked right into the trap and had certainly not engaged brain before opening mouth. I was quickly bowing and scraping and desperately trying to claw myself out of the mire.

In the 19th and early 20th centuries most forces required that recruits be at least 5 feet 10 inches (178 cm) in height. Nottingham City Police had a minimum height requirement of 6 feet but by 1960 many forces had reduced this to 5 feet 8 inches (173 cm), and 5 feet 4 inches (163 cm) for women. It was in fact, the 1999 MacPherson report that recommended against height restrictions, arguing that they may discriminate against those of ethnic backgrounds who are genetically predisposed to be shorter than average. By the way, it was also the same report which described the Metropolitan Police as 'Institutionally Racist'.

There are currently no minimum or maximum height requirements to join the police force. Apart from graduate entry schemes as mentioned earlier, there are no formal educational requirements for recruitment to the police service, but without the 'A' levels mentioned, applicants must take two written tests to ensure they have a reasonable standard of English, as well as a numeracy test.

So, this was another major change in the shape of policing. Although police officers now have modern communications equipment and can respond to problem calls far quicker in their vehicles often with two or more officers aboard, I'm still of the belief that the image of the police has deteriorated considerably now that the height of the 'old-time' bobbies would see them tower over their more modern 'shorter' brothers and sisters. Of course, if they're not wearing their headdress, and with their black open necked shirts, then they'll look a lot worse.

General Appearances

When I see officers now wearing 'HI Viz jackets and 'Stab Proof' vests, with their belts from which many additional pieces of kit must be carried, I thank my lucky stars that I was only required to carry my truncheon in my truncheon pocket, (never struck in anger) my rarely used handcuffs on the back of my belt and a whistle, (never blown in anger) and my pocket book carried in my tunic's breast pocket.

Changing times may be the reason why it is now important to wear stab / bullet proof vests and special belts to carry such items as tasers, extended batons, an Airwave radio / telephone, incapacitant spray, ear pieces and a variety of first aid items.

However, very often the officers carrying them are without their headgear and ties and I wonder whether those on foot patrol could be forgiven for not carrying a lot of this equipment if they were in knowledge of the rapid response of their mobile colleagues who of course, would have on board just about everything they might require in a tight corner.

The roll-out of the 'Airwave' radios at around the turn of the century provided a secure, digital radio network and telephone which conversely reduced the size and weight of the heavier, hitherto much larger 'two-part' Pye radios carried in my day.

In addition to some officers being shorter, they are often seen with tattoos, earrings or wearing other jewellery. In addition, beards and hair grown over the collar have become the norm but in my day, even beards were not permitted unless grown for medical reasons. Also, tattoos visible were not permitted and those who joined with them, were required to keep them covered even when 'short sleeve order' was permitted.

I can hear the cries —"Yes, but we live in a different era".

I'm fully aware of the different times we're in and I suppose us old soldiers need to bend a little but I can't help but feel that we are losing out a little on respect in that regard. Indeed, this was a subject I put to a Chief Inspector in another force recently who agreed that appearance of officers these days are much more relaxed and embracing of difference - tattoos, hairstyles, piercings, headgear etc. The officer was of the impression that this was a positive aspect because officers will be looking more like the communities in which they serve.

This observation came very soon after I had also discussed it with a fellow dinosaur. I put my observations to him and he mentioned that whilst passing two female officers without hats, he couldn't resist politely asking them why they were not wearing them. The one responded by saying, "It makes us more acceptable in the community, Sir".

Having received both comments in the same month, I have to ask myself if that can be remotely correct; maybe I am out of sync with the times but are these times correct and in fact, does that really make them more respected by the community? Is there a need to dress down so that we look like the community, and if so, does that mean that respect or acceptance of it, can only be earned by 'dressing down'? I don't think so. Quite the reverse, I would say. The fact remains that in my view, and many (OK fellow dinosaurs) who I have discussed this with, believe that our police officers do not command the respect they were once used to because of such appearances.

The photograph below of a c1900 officer, is as good as I can find which displays something of the smartness expected; although his tunic looks like new issue the sleeves are too long; perhaps he got it off the 'hand me down' reserves I used to look after in the attic at Herefordshire's Police Headquarters? His trousers are also absent of a visible crease but there again, the photograph has all the hallmarks of it being set up with models. It does, however, show off the officer's fine bearing. I wonder if he had a stop and search' ticket to issue to this man after he had searched his 'poachers bag' and his rather bulky overcoat?

A Victorian Constable c1900 – Courtesy of WyrdLight.com under licence

Other than his motif bedecked truncheon which is longer than the one I carried; I cannot see any signs of further appointments which he was expected to carry.

The above photograph taken from a 'Throwback Thursday' article depicting the old and new police in Gloucester, demonstrates more clearly, the amount of equipment required to be carried by today's officers and maybe that, in itself, is the problem. The image of the 'old bobby' is probably a more realistic one also, especially the size of his girth, but of course, as usual, it is so easy to type cast all into these images when indeed, all were not like that at all.

So far as dress and equipment is concerned, others will have a contrary view but I cannot believe that the carrying of this equipment, (normally in police vehicles anyway) can justify the absence of wearing the items of clothing, which, after all, had become the hallmark for the excellent reputation which our police service had earned over many years. I feel that the patrolling officers' helmets will soon become a museum item to be replaced by baseball type caps and what a sad day that will be.

The duties of specialist officers for example 'Authorised Firearms Officers' (AFO's) Dog Handlers, Polsa trained searchers and 'Task Force' type policing does make such garments more practical to wear. However, for as long as the 'beat patrol' officer survives extinction, 'no thank you', as far as I'm concerned.

I came across this above photograph in the 'West Mercia Memories' private Facebook website which is compiled and read by current, but mostly past officers. It seems possible that it was taken and published by the officers of this police station to show that they were all wearing face coverings in response to the 'Covid 19' Pandemic. Full marks for that but why didn't they think about what else they were wearing? The photograph drew numerous negative comments about their shabby appearance. (So, it's not just me!!)

Yes, I can also recall in our much 'poorer' days when free fish and chips were generously provided as were the Chinese or Indian meals free of charge, eaten within the kitchen areas of these establishments when on duty. But these gifts which, of course, were received completely in contravention of 'Police Discipline' Regulations, were received in a subtle way, but never in public view. It goes without saying that many public houses were visited and supervised from mostly the rear private rooms, out of view out of mind and with jug in hand.

I mention this again only to compare the subtle ways in which such practices were performed. In these more modern days, I would be surprised if such goods were asked for, let alone being received for free at all, but the point I wish to make is that frequently, I have witnessed hatless officers, often parking their vehicles where they shouldn't, alight to enter shops to conduct what I can only believe is their shopping. I have witnessed them leave these shops eating chocolate bars etc. which they would have just purchased. It just doesn't look right for many reasons. These changing shapes of policing, are for me, definitely 'NOT GOOD ONES'.

8.

ORGANISATION AND STRUCTURE

The Olden Days

Whilst I'm only really concerned with the shape of the organisational and structural changes of the modern era, particularly since 1960, it is as well to reflect a little as to how we reached that point.

There were, of course, many different ways in which the peace was protected even before the days of Robert Peel, the 'Bow Street Runners' and the inception of what we now know as the Metropolitan Police in 1829. Other small towns and boroughs followed suit and even when I joined the Herefordshire Constabulary in 1960, I can recall hearing conversations on subjects about what had been the Hereford City Police. Indeed, the police force in the small town of Leominster, located about 14 miles north of Hereford, had also evolved at the same time in 1836, as the Hereford City police.

The Municipal Corporations Act of 1835, had directed that cities and towns which possessed a Royal Charter, were to create Watch Committees with a responsibility to form police forces for their areas. They were also to oversee the management and funding of them. Running in tandem with those forward strides, a year later a County Commission on the payment of rates, made a scathing report on the parochial police throughout England and Wales. This led to many additional 'City' and 'Borough' police forces being inaugurated.

When compared with the chapters of history in other spheres, it is surprising to discover that not a great deal of change has been witnessed in the 'policing sphere' since the passing of those days. The need for larger geographical shapes of organisation was recognised to run in parallel with growths of population and economies.

Leaping forward a while to more modern times, police stations were built in most villages of England and Wales. In the Ledbury town area where I first worked as a police officer in 1960, this small market town was surrounded by six or eight village police stations. Colwall, Much Marcle, Tarrington, Cradley and Bosbury are just a few that I can remember.

Most all were policed on foot or pedal cycles until way into the 1960s when low powered motorcycles were issued to some. In our case, it was those silent ghosts called Velocettes. They were almost equivalent in fashion that the sit up and beg type pedal cycles were to modern day racers. They would never have featured in the Isle of Man TT races. Indeed, such a machine was the first motorcycle I was to later own. It was water cooled and had a lever on the side which was necessary to pull, in order to start it.

Whilst on night duty in 1963, I recall being in The Homend, Ledbury which is the main road running into and out of the town, when I became aware of a dark shadowy figure riding a cycle towards me. It must have been late at night; maybe even past midnight and the cyclist was riding out of town. The speed of the bike being pedalled up the gradient, just managed to keep the dynamo alive and flickering the headlamp alight. As it drew closer I could identify the helmet, cape and uniform of one of our village officers, on his way back to what was his home and his police station in the village of Bosbury.

He had another five or so miles to push his bike along the pitch-black country lanes he faced once leaving this road only about half a mile ahead of him. He hadn't been at the Police Station when I had started my shift and so far as I knew, although he had a 24-hour duty responsibility, there had not been any reason for him to have been in Ledbury at all. With no firm evidence to the contrary, I could only surmise that he had spent some time in the back of one of our licensed premises. (Supervising of course!) In most cases, it was no use applying for a village beat if you couldn't hold your drink!

The point of me mentioning all this was to draw a picture of police coverage in readers' minds. This Ledbury Sub Division spread far and wide over a huge rural area all the way to the borders with our sister, Sub Division at Ross on Wye and all the way to the Divisional boundaries with its neighbouring Divisions at Hereford and Malvern and on the one side, the county boundary with Gloucestershire. This meant that in addition to all urban areas, every inch of the rural areas in between, were adequately covered by rural village beat officers.

When on duty, these officers had 24-hour responsibility for their areas and so this ensured that every field of the rural countryside was policed by them. However, the towns and city urban areas with their populations grew, and the housing requirements which followed, saw estates being built on the periphery of the urban area. So far as policing these estates were concerned, the residents of them were caught in the gap between the urban areas of the cities or town boundaries and the wider rural villages.

The common-sense solution saw the building of police houses on these estates as they were being built so that the officers resident in them could be utilised to police the immediate area where they lived. These were called 'Resident Beats' and the officers living in them, 'Resident Beat Officers. (RBOs) or Local Beat Officers (LBOs) Whilst the policing advantages of such a strategy are self-evident, so far as living on them was concerned, many of the estates were unpopular and troublesome areas where one wouldn't perhaps, have otherwise chosen to live. But, of course, the Police Regulations of the day, directed that Chief Constables could direct officers, usually with little resistance, to live wherever they wanted them to live.

The 'pay off' concerned the free occupation of these police houses, so, *'what was good for the goose, became good for the gander'* and the provision of police houses for occupation by officers, not even responsible for policing these areas, became the norm. What's more, if officers had been lucky enough to purchase their own properties (in City or Borough forces only) or rent them privately, they would be recompensed financially with a payment called a 'Rent Allowance', which was paid in our monthly pay cheques. The amounts were calculated by a comparison of the rateable value of one selected police house compared with that of the private premises they occupied.

It was always intended that the rent allowance be paid 'tax free' but the Inland Revenue disagreed with that concept, so an annual repayment of the tax paid, was made which was termed, a 'Compensatory Grant'. This made the salary payment for that particular month, very worthwhile indeed and officers frequently used it to help finance an annual holiday, which otherwise was beyond their finances.

The story was often told that, as some police wives weren't familiar with this grant, when they saw the term, 'Compensatory Grant' written on a pay slip, they asked their husbands what it meant, the reply was, **"Oh don't worry about that dear, I'll pay it"**! I trust that wasn't a true story.

Perhaps it isn't fair to suggest that this 'pay off' was equal to all because guess what, as mentioned a few paragraphs above, with Chief Officers of Police being able to direct their officers to live in any place of their choosing within the force area, they probably had the best side of that deal.

Being 'sent' to a rural outpost or a troublesome estate, was often a discipline tactic exercised by my old Chief Constable, Alex Rennie. That tactic could not, of course, apply to City or Borough forces as their places of duty would not extend beyond their short boundaries.

This estate and village policing structure meant that it would only be necessary for an urban officer to attend these 'out of town' areas in the division's police van due to the unavailability of village constables or the RBOs who may be on leave or on a rest day. In addition, they would also respond to provide any back up required. The fact that prior to 1967, we only possessed one such vehicle will be further explained in the chapter below.

RBOs and Village Policemen were selected from those who had tucked a good few years of police service under their belts and weren't particularly looking to move house for promotion. So, what could possibly go wrong?

Thank goodness that such enforced moves are normally things of the past, and it is most unlikely that officers will be refused a move into their own premises, plus the fact that if chief officers now want to post officers from one location to another, without the police accommodation previously available, these situations make it very costly for forces to pay the expenses caused by such moves and therefore, the occurrences when this does unusually happen, are far less prevalent these days.

So, who is left to police the outer estates and country villages today? We do actually see a small police car travel through our village on sparse occasions, but I have never witnessed the occupant/s parking up or interacting in any way with the villagers. Even though we have been provided with the name of a particular constable and contact details in our monthly newsletter, I have never seen or met him despite attempting on two occasions to meet him.

It was during my research with a Police and Community Support Officer that I mentioned this to her and subsequently, she responded and informed me that he had attempted to contact me to no avail? I continue to receive contact from the PCSO.

9.

RESTRICTIONS ON PRIVATE LIVES

So, for people not hitherto involved with the Police Service, I feel that they may be a little surprised to be enlightened about the scope of discipline and other intrusions into our private lives that we were required to endure. They were extended to lengths far beyond that experienced by most other employees involved in other occupations.

For a start, in order to impose these restrictions on us, they were enshrined in statute law in the form of Statutory Instruments named 'Police Regulations' which dominated the way we worked and lived and which were constantly being amended and replaced with later versions as and when it became necessary.

As might be expected, they were framed completely on the side of our employer's governance which meant it was 'one way' traffic and never much in our favour. Of course, they were seen as being necessary, otherwise we might lose the pride we held in being the police which the community deserved, a microcosm within a democracy as opposed to being a political puppet not unlike other less democratic countries.

After all, they were designed to prevent officers discrediting themselves or their constabularies. In my day, they directed a multitude of actions or conduct which, if breached, could result in disciplinary action ranging from being cautioned to being fined or even being dismissed from the service, indeed, those sanctions remain today.

I shall refer to many as we plough through this book but those that which readily jump out at me after all this time, which for me, had hit us harder than most, include: -

- Not gaining employment in any other occupation.
- Not to own or be involved in the running of any other business.
- Being made to reside in accommodation and at locations only approved by the Police Authority through the Chief of Police.
- Not to accept any gift or favour.
- Not to marry without the consent of the Chief Constable and then only to approved potential spouses.
- To report the births of any child born to their relationships

In addition to these statutory restrictions, each Chief Constable was permitted to make their own 'General or Standing Orders' which in effect, served to add any further restrictions desired. One wonders where this draconian power could end, but in my own force, our Chief Constable, Alex Rennie, was very strict indeed. His sternness not only included the severity of his punishments, but the additional nature of his specific directives. A good example of this related to appearance, particularly the growth of beards. He directed that they looked scruffy and hence declared that they would not be worn unless with a medical certificate. Some officers felt so strongly about this, that they transferred to other forces where they were permitted to grow beards.

In county forces, not being able to purchase our own homes, even in the unlikely event that we could afford to, was a huge burden. This restriction was eventually relaxed at various times but over the years and depending on the Chief Constable, only when retirement was on the horizon but then, at the other end of the spectrum in more recent years, officers have been permitted to travel very long distances from home to work. Indeed, I'm aware that a Superintendent I know, once travelled from Bidford on Avon to Northamptonshire at least a 100-mile round trip. Then, after transferring to Thames Valley Police and moving house, he was still able to travel around 30 miles to his place of work.

Such relaxation must be welcomed if it means that it will not obstruct the officers from performing their duties in any way. It might well mean an inconvenience which must be accepted, should they be required to return to duty, maybe on more than one occasion on the same day, as this officer I refer to, had indeed experienced. Such flexibility was welcomed and I suppose that even though the travel costs would be at the officer's own expense, in the longer term it suited domestic circumstances and was probably less of a financial burden than moving location. In any event, I guess the acid test was whether these travelling officers could manage to report on time for their duties as and when required. I mention it only to draw the comparisons in the tolerance of these regulations which have served to change the shape of policing today.

Other restrictions were designed as preventive measures in stopping us becoming obligated to people who may wish to use such positions for their own benefits.

Asking permission to marry a named potential spouse so that they and their families' background could be vetted, was obviously a huge intrusion into our family lives. I can actually remember some pertinent questions being asked of one officer concerning his proposed marriage to a lady from a 'known' family. The marriage occurred in the end and obviously, if there were no skeletons in the cupboard, then there was nothing to worry about. (I smile here, because it was not until after I retired when I engaged in the hobby of genealogy, that I discovered that two of my maternal grandmother's siblings had been imprisoned for making and passing forged one-pound notes!)

But no, this was not in the Middle-Ages and believe it or not, as for my own marriage to Josephine Williams was concerned, it wasn't only her father, who gave me permission to marry his daughter, the Chief Constable also had to nod his head. It was also a requirement for us to report the births of any of our children but in fairness, it was also during my time that these requirements were watered down to just becoming necessary for the updating of personal records for the payment of pensions and rent allowance purposes etc. But our domestic circumstances were, however, hit in later years when I had crept up to the Inspector rank. (When no one was looking!)

In the mid-1970s, my wife became very interested in the purchase of a small hairdressing salon near to where we lived and indeed, her father was prepared to help finance such a venture. It was always possible to have another income stream with permission from the Chief Constables but my experience of such permissions being given, was very rare. There were ways of avoiding being caught and I knew others who had set up businesses, one in particular whose wife ran a café in Hereford. He was never taken to task about it because he was never caught, or could it have been blind eyes that were applied?

Placing businesses in relatives names was a useless idea anyway, because the regulation also covered the interest in or ownerships of businesses owned by relatives, so whilst that might help to keep the business interest under wraps, it wouldn't help if it was discovered. That was taking a risk I wasn't prepared to accept, indeed, placing the business in Jo's fathers name would have been an option but I knew that if I was to progress further, then we would be having to face the prospect of moving from that location. All in all, it was decided that we would drop the idea completely.

Thank goodness, that since my retirement, Police Regulations have, to some extent, evolved to be less restrictive than those earlier more repressive ones and reflect more closely to modern day times and living.

Almost coinciding with my retirement, the 1995 Regulations prescribed for part time employment, job sharing and career breaks. These schemes would not have even been considered back in the 1960s or indeed not many years before they became a reality. Since then, further changes were made by the 2003 Regulations and more recently in Schedule 2 of The Police (Conduct) Regulations 2020. The shape of policing constantly changes.

This latest statute largely reflects changes made to the handling of police complaints and police disciplinary matters made by the Policing and Crime Act 2017 (2017 c. 3). However, in connection with the behaviour of police officers, Schedule 2 of the statute deals with standards of professional behaviour and lists the following: -

1. **Honesty and Integrity.** - Police officers are honest, act with integrity and do not compromise or abuse their position.

2. **Authority, Respect and Courtesy.** - Police officers act with self-control and tolerance, treating members of the public and colleagues with respect and courtesy. Police officers do not abuse their powers or authority and respect the rights of all individuals.

3. **Equality and Diversity.** - Police officers act with fairness and impartiality. They do not discriminate unlawfully or unfairly.

4. **Use of Force.** - Police officers only use force to the extent that it is necessary, proportionate and reasonable in all the circumstances.

5. **Orders and Instructions** - Police officers only give and carry out lawful orders and instructions. Police officers abide by police regulations, force policies and lawful orders.

6. **Duties and Responsibilities** - Police officers are diligent in the exercise of their duties and responsibilities. Police officers have a responsibility to give appropriate cooperation during investigations, inquiries and formal proceedings, participating openly and professionally in line with the expectations of a police officer when identified as a witness.

7. **Confidentiality.** - Police officers treat information with respect and access or disclose it only in the proper course of police duties.

8. **Fitness for Duty.** - Police officers when on duty or presenting themselves for duty are fit to carry out their responsibilities.

9. **Discreditable Conduct.** - Police officers behave in a manner which does not discredit the police service or undermine public confidence in it, whether on or off duty.
   Police officers report any action taken against them for a criminal offence, any conditions imposed on them by a court or the receipt of any penalty notice.

10. **Challenging and Reporting Improper Conduct.** - Police officers report, challenge or take action against the conduct of colleagues which has fallen below the Standards of Professional Behaviour.

This latter 'Whistleblowing' regulation could have caused riots if applied in the earlier days of my career. Regulations being so strict at the minor level, there could have been many 'tit for tat' occasions which if applied, would have caused ructions. Hence, such a regulation was not even considered – perhaps it should have been but its non-compliance would make its introduction a waste of time.

Though still covered by specific regulations, the regulations listed above are the broad objectives that are willingly carried on officer's shoulders, in most cases with pride. They are now more widely encompassing but are probably more effective than the previous, more prescriptive regulations.

So, these later provisions have finally been arrived at through many amendments in legislation and in more modern times, they have been shaped in targeting more serious aspects of corruption but at the same time, have put into place a more common-sense framework which has led to the overall shape of policing in a more suitable environment for today's policing activities. The relaxing of the restrictions to private lives could have been made much sooner.

So far as officers are concerned, the one advantage I can see immediately unfortunately concerns the selling off of village police stations and resident beat houses which have resulted in the nation's policing resources being centred in urban conurbations. Disaster for the rural communities maybe, but from another perspective, no longer can our Chief Officers forcibly post officers to these often, far flung locations which may have been the least desirable places which one might have wanted their families to be.

I guess also, that with an ounce of common sense being thrown in, it finally reflected that we were living in more enlightened times.

Complaints against the Police

Complaints made against police officers were also similarly formalised as many resulted from allegations of police misconduct. In my day, it was the Police Complaints Authority who, with various force Complaints and Discipline Departments, some later re-named 'Professional Standards' departments, managed such issues with Deputy Chief Constables at the helm of them.

Police investigating their own officers was, however, and always will be a subject of concern. The rules I served under were under the umbrella of the independent 'Police Complaints Authority'. This agency then gave way to the 'Independent Police Complaints Commission' (IPCC) which was introduced to oversee the investigations. The current agency changed in 2018 and is now governed by the Independent Office for Police Conduct. (IOPC)

Among many changed procedures, additional measures were required to tighten and improve investigations into police corruption. It is interesting to note, however, that in a review published by the IPCC, the overriding message coming out of the report was: -

'That corruption is not widespread, or considered to be widespread, but that where it exists it is corrosive of the public trust that is at the heart of policing by consent. Public confidence in and acceptance of the police exercising their considerable powers over us all is heavily dependent on a belief in the integrity of individual officers. That legitimacy is called into question and undermined by the kinds of behaviour described in this report, and by any attempts to justify or minimise behaviour that the ordinary citizen sees as corrupt – accepting generous hospitality, gaining personal benefit or abusing powers for personal gain – particularly when this is carried out or apparently condoned at senior levels'.

Complaints were investigated mostly by Senior Police Officers of the Superintendent ranks but as time progressed and a system of informally resolving the issues was introduced, that requirement was relaxed when many were dealt with by lower ranks, mainly by Chief Inspectors. I conducted many of these myself in both ranks.

Despite any changes in procedure, I am convinced that the public will, however, never ever accept that the police policing themselves, is a good idea. Of course, on the face of it, it isn't a good idea but let me at least try to dispel their concern and convince those who doubt the integrity of this practice, that in my view, it would be extremely difficult to find a method which completely discounts any current officer from at least assisting with a complaint or discipline investigation and also, that any other investigator would not be better equipped to arrive at the same level of investigative professionalism as police officers.

I cannot speak for all others but would say that the urge to get to the bottom of such things is inherent in all investigators and if that means throwing a bad apple out of a barrel, then that can only be a good thing.

Current complaint investigations can be dealt with entirely by the Independent Office for Police Conduct or internally or a mixture of the two, whichever they direct. Having retired from the force I felt honoured and privileged to have been invited back by the then Deputy Chief Constable, to examine the procedures used in the force under the Police Complaints authority and then to design a system which would convert that into the new requirements of the incoming 'Independent Police Complaints Commission' – (IPCC). This was as a paid consultancy and not under the force's 'Retained Experienced Personnel' scheme.

The negative aspects of complaint investigations by senior officers who are not part of a force's 'Professional Standards' Departments is better explained with my own experiences, as a Superintendent and Chief Superintendent.

The major 'downside' concerns the fact that in addition to conducting these investigations, I was having to perform my normal duties. No sooner had I completed one, I would be issued with another. It seemed to me that I was receiving more of the difficult complaint investigations, which were often against senior officers in other forces.

One particular case I recall was given to me on 18th June 1981, following the disappearance of the managing director of The Dunlop Rubber Company at the Birmingham based 'Fort Dunlop' headquarters, his body was found in a decomposed state in some woods near Henley on Thames. He resided in Shipston on Stour, Warwickshire which was approximately mid-way between his Birmingham Headquarters and another Dunlop Company situated in Brynmawr, South Wales.

His widow complained against the Warwickshire Constabulary officers assigned to his disappearance for being negligent in their 'Missing Person' enquiries and also against other Thames Valley Officers who dealt with his death. In addition, she divulged that her husband had informed her that another member of the Dunlop board of directors was in the process of blackmailing him. She strongly suspected that it was this board member who had murdered him. As dubious as these claims might appear to be, they obviously were required to be taken seriously.

This was going to be a long and protracted enquiry and I selected a rugby team colleague of the past, a Chief Inspector to assist me. It was not completed until over 12 months from the time I received it.

Without going into detail, that year was very busy indeed. I had operational commitments including royal visits, our defences against the IRA attacks on the mainland with myself organising terrorism exercises and many other operational matters. I guess the time taken could have been reduced by well over 50% had it not been for other commitments. Indeed, there came a time after a year had elapsed, when the Deputy Chief Constable of Thames Valley

Police summoned me to his office and put me on notice that he wanted my report as soon as possible.

As an aside, it was on route to answer my summons from the Deputy, that some bright spark rammed right into the rear of my stationary car which I had stopped at the rear of others, to allow a vehicle ahead of us to turn right. It occurred in Gloucestershire and although the driver of the vehicle immediately admitted liability, the police attendance and the making of the report and my statement, caused me to have to adjourn my meeting to another date, causing even more delay.

But such were the allegations made by the complainant, it became necessary for us to, in effect, conduct a murder enquiry in retrospect and due to the blackmail allegation, this entailed an audit of exactly what her husband did with his very large income. That audit made it clear that unbeknown to any of his family, friends or work colleagues, including his private secretary who managed his drinks cabinet under lock and key, that a huge amount of money was being spent on alcohol.

No-one connected with him, to this day would believe me but it soon transpired that we were building a file in order to prove such things, as opposed to proving that he had been blackmailed and murdered. Nothing else would have satisfied his wife who continued to write to me for many years afterwards, suggesting that I had made a corrupt investigation.

Sadly, his body was so decomposed that his identity was not easily ascertained, nor was the cause of his death. Also sadly, there were clues left at his scene of death, some of which were destroyed by weather and animals, that could have thrown light on both issues. There were many things which indeed, supported her allegations but which, if dealt with more professionally, would have prevented her complaints being made in the first place and certainly, in a less vociferous tone.

My report indicated the suspicion that his allegations of being blackmailed were made in an attempt to divert his wife from suspicions about his spending an extortionate amount of money on alcohol. We were able to prove that all the indications were, that he eventually committed suicide by taking drugs from his wife's possession. (She was a district nurse) He had taken a bottle of whiskey into the woods, sat down on a newspaper and swallowed the lot.

The investigation and scene management of his death was inevitably lacking and officers received admonishments over this aspect of policing. I later received a letter of thanks and appreciation for the 'in depth' investigation which satisfied the Police Complaints Authority who wrote to both forces commending my report to them.

Another example which came around ten years later was against a force's Detective Chief Superintendent and it involved allegations of sloppy work in connection with an investigation into the death of a young man, a university undergraduate whose charred and unrecognisable body had been found not too far away from his home, in suspicious circumstances. On this occasion, I was assisted by the Detective Chief Inspector of our Worcester Division who again, found it difficult to absent himself from his 'number one' responsibilities.

The investigation took many months to complete and like the previous example, it meant frequently travelling to and from the force area and in this case, to the deceased's university at Hull.

The below body of the letter minus the force's letterhead identity was received from the Deputy Chief Constable of the force concerned to my own Deputy Chief is atypical of communications received from Police Complaints Authority members and I don't mind recording the appreciation I gained in reading their comments.

The Detective Chief Superintendent concerned handed me his resignation at the conclusion of my interview with him. I felt some sympathy for him because he was a member of one of the smaller type forces and the lack of resources played its part.

The problem with receiving such accolades was twofold. Other officers were obviously required to carry out my normal duties whilst I was away. The complaint investigations were made by me when I could ill afford the time to be absent from my home force and it was a good job that I had an excellent deputy to watch my back but it certainly was also an imposition on him.

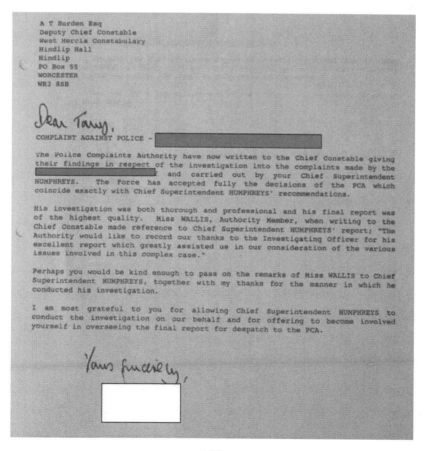

A T Burden Esq
Deputy Chief Constable
West Mercia Constabulary
Hindlip Hall
Hindlip
PO Box 55
WORCESTER
WR3 8SB

Dear Tony,

COMPLAINT AGAINST POLICE -

The Police Complaints Authority have now written to the Chief Constable giving their findings in respect of the investigation into the complaints made by the ████████████ and carried out by your Chief Superintendent HUMPHREYS. The Force has accepted fully the decisions of the PCA which coincide exactly with Chief Superintendent HUMPHREYS' recommendations.

His investigation was both thorough and professional and his final report was of the highest quality. Miss WALLIS, Authority Member, when writing to the Chief Constable made reference to Chief Superintendent HUMPHREYS' report; "The Authority would like to record our thanks to the Investigating Officer for his excellent report which greatly assisted us in our consideration of the various issues involved in this complex case."

Perhaps you would be kind enough to pass on the remarks of Miss WALLIS to Chief Superintendent HUMPHREYS, together with my thanks for the manner in which he conducted his investigation.

I am most grateful to you for allowing Chief Superintendent HUMPHREYS to conduct the investigation on our behalf and for offering to become involved yourself in overseeing the final report for despatch to the PCA.

Yours sincerely,

The other downside led to similar conclusions in that it wasn't very long after conducting my first investigation in another police force, before I received other complaints to investigate outside of my own force. This imposition into my 'day job' was such that it must have affected what I was doing.

So overall, whilst changes may have been made for the better, I strongly believe that there should be resources made available for forces to deploy specialised teams for such protracted complaints against the police investigations so as not to impinge on further disruption to the main duties to which senior officers are assigned. Such postings would also not be long term ones but whatever, other duties should not be required to be performed at the same time.

Once again, I can hear the shouts of **"Where are we going to find the resources"?** I can imagine the problems and they will not be solved by ministers reducing the ranks of officers by 20,000 at a time as has been recently witnessed – it is the government's responsibility to provide such resources and provide them, they should!

Whilst I have not been involved under current methods of the supervision of public complaints, the criticism levelled at the police of policing their own is, as far as I'm aware, ill founded. It is my belief that all investigators will want to do the best job that they can and receiving that criticism will only mean that in any event, they would want to prove it wrong.

Sadly, one of the criticisms raised against Cressida Dick concerns her being obstructive in preventing easy access to documents and computer information in the 'Morgan' murder, now challenge my beliefs. As I write, the investigation has yet to be concluded and I truly hope they are wrong but would applaud the truth, if they are found to be substantiated. I can only assume that changes made have been for the good until I'm proven wrong.

10.

METHODS OF POLICE OPERATIONS

So for those who may have reached this point in my book and have arrived at the conclusion that I have been tinkering around the periphery of the major changes and causes in policing practices I have witnessed, let me assure them that I have not forgotten why they are closest to my heart. These involve the obstructions however worthy they may appear, to have caused our police investigations to more often fail to arrive at justice in our courts. I think now is the time when we should be reminded of one of those definitions I was required to learn parrot fashion 61 years ago.

'A constable is a citizen locally appointed but having authority under the Crown for the protection of life and property, the prevention and detection of crime, the maintenance of order, and the prosecution of offenders against the peace'.

I'm proud to have remembered it by heart, and although I felt sure that it wouldn't have changed since then, I have to admit that I've checked it, and it hasn't.

Although the words hold very true, the different ways and the energy expended so as to be in compliance with that definition, have long been overtaken in my estimation.

The below are examples where, in my view, operating procedures have been re-shaped to negatively impact on our objective to fully comply with that definition.

Briefing Parades

Before I get my teeth into my pet subjects such as 'no comment' interviews, and other meatier aspects of general policing and crime investigations, let me first deal with other peripheral aspects. These I consider in the long term have had an effect on such things and have had a detrimental effect to the successful apprehension of criminals in the first place.

The idea of how towns and cities were policed in the early sixties was that the vast majority of our policemen were given a briefing lasting a full fifteen minutes before they started their shift and by each then walking (once being marched) to their allotted beats. Albeit not realised by the majority of us, this briefing was in our own time until the Police Federation (our union) got a hold on it.

Most beats were foot beats in the centres of these towns or cities and the outer area, or the commercial outskirts, were patrolled on pedal cycles. No radios were available to be issued and with only the barest means of communications, which I shall deal with below, meant that you were very much on your own. Beat officers were not permitted to leave the beats allocated unless an emergency arose or normally by appointment made with the Sergeant for such things as completing administration at the police station. (Report writing).

It was of course, very much frowned upon should anyone report late for the briefing. The early turn shift commencing at 6am required attendance at the station at 5.45am, a duty hated by all. With only two of us on a shift at Ledbury, this was not necessary as the shift we were about to relieve, would let us know about anything worth knowing. Any noteworthy occurrence would have been made subject of an entry in the General Occurrence Book (GOB) and this together with Crime information and the 'Process Book' (those who had been booked) would have been read through prior to our patrol, and that was about it.

On nights, you could add to that, a need to look at the vacant premises register; a register indicating where those who could afford it, generally the upper crust, had valuables to protect and would expect their premises to be visited now and again through the night. Modern day officers will now be falling off their seats with laughter as one might expect.

The police stations at Hereford and Worcester, were quite different and one couldn't remain in the station for a minute later than the hour our shift commenced. We had already been in the station for fifteen minutes for our briefing. The sergeant would have been there even earlier because he had to decide who was going to work specific beats and needed to have updated himself with the details of any intelligence he felt was likely to assist us in the execution of our duties, as defined in the opening paragraphs of this chapter.

Indeed, in addition to our pocket notebooks, we were also issued with another book specifically designed to record stolen vehicles so that quick references to the registration numbers was provided. (What a great change automatic number plate recording would have brought)

The sergeant would ensure that everything on the *message pad* worth knowing was discussed on parade. It was this message pad which was eventually made redundant when personal computers came into being. At Hereford, all messages worth reading and sharing were circulated after being typed out on a form B22, mainly by 'Station Duty Officers' timed and dated and which were then added to the message pad in chronological order.

These forms contained details of every telephone message of operational substance. For example, all crimes reported would warrant a separate message for circulation. We called them 1 to 6s because they were made up of six points.

1 The classification of the crime,

2 Where it occurred,

3 The times it had occurred between,

4 The Modus Operandi (MO),

5 Details of stolen property or persons injured etc. and finally,

6 Details of any suspects sought.

Today, such information is contained within a computer and hence more rapidly circulated on forces' 'Command and Control' systems. Of course, no hard copy is produced and left lying around on a clipboard as it was; so unless one now logs into these computers, officers would not become aware of such important matters.

Whilst technology has undoubtedly played a part, the details of such vital information will not have been accessed other than during duty time. My recent research reveals however, that at least the parading sergeants are still reporting earlier (without extra pay) to get ahead of the game and in order to brief their shift.

Research in another force indicates that some form of briefing does indeed, occur at the beginning of a shift, i.e. at the start of duty time but not before it. However, with officers about to terminate their shift at the same time, this will surely leave areas bereft of police cover? Whilst agreeing that a briefing time would be an opportunity to build a sense of 'team', I was informed that should an immediate call for s response be received, officers would leave that briefing.

Modern day technology is such that some material can be delivered by screens and mapping systems. In addition, intelligence departments provide a daily product, much like our collators did when the fifteen-minute briefing period was cast to the wind.

Forces, wealthier than ours, employed Station Sergeants to operate at front desks but at Hereford, we had senior constables, often suffering from some medical condition or other, who performed this duty and so, it more often than not, fell to them to receive such messages and to type them out. For that reason, the pad would mostly be found behind the front desk where the station duty officer (SDO) had his typewriter and where he greeted visitors to the station. (Or threw them out!)

In order to get ahead of the game, the temptation was to gather around the pad and read it with others with the same idea. The parade room was right next to the public enquiry area and separated by a door with a glass panel in the upper half. It was easier to read it there instead of taking it into the parade room but that became a nuisance for the SDO and it was not very conducive for the public to see this scrum of officers or indeed, for the SDO to carry out his duties.

My thanks go to my mate, Chris Furber, who reminds me about a story regarding this and which involved that 'posh' sounding Sergeant, Selwyn Roberts as mentioned earlier. The Superintendent of the day, had issued a memorandum to the effect that such gatherings would not occur at the 'Enquiry Desk' and the message pad should be taken into the parade room for the briefing.

However, it wasn't long before the Superintendent himself visited the Enquiry Office to have a look at the pad. The door between it and the parade room was locked and so he rapped on the glass panel demanding it be opened for access to the pad which was with the SDO. From the other side of the door, Selwyn had stuck a copy of the memo against the glass pane and pointing to it, mimed to him his apologies in the best Oxford accent he could muster, "Very sorry sir, must obey orders" or words similar.

Unbeknown to Selwyn, the Superintendent, John Keyte had not long before, had a memo drafted relative his search for a Sergeant to transfer to one of the most undesirable and distant rural outcrops of Herefordshire, such a posting not fancied by anyone. So, it wasn't long after he returned to the door and attracting Selwyn's attention to the memo, which he had pressed against the window, he mimed, "Read This". The door was opened in double quick time with both sporting a smirk on their faces. That incident was typical of the humour of our small force and which was conducive to it being referred to as a 'family' type of force. John Keyte had played an integral part in my career and was well regarded by many of us.

So this fifteen-minute briefing session was very important and on 'early turn' shift (6am to 2pm) waking and then dragging myself out of bed was very difficult indeed. When at school and in the school rowing crew, I needed to rise early to go for my run, often in the dark before getting changed to bike across the river to deliver papers about two miles away from home. I then needed to return to get changed for school and bike another two miles to get there. No wonder I often felt like sleeping instead of learning!

But PC 157 Jim Whent obviously had a bigger problem than most because too frequently, he would arrive after the briefing had started. I recall one occasion when he was taken to task by the briefing sergeant when he gave the most bizarre explanation. It went something like –

"Well Serge, I have this one deaf ear you see. I always set my alarm and sleep on my deaf ear so that I will hear the alarm go off. Unfortunately, during the night, I must turn over onto my good ear and it stops me from hearing the alarm".

We were doubled up with laughter but our humour needed to be tempered somewhat as the sergeant might well have thought that we were 'taking the Mick'! So, some bright spark had the brilliant idea of forging a memorandum from the Chief Constable which directed that Jim must attend the Police Surgeon's practice at a specific time and date for the purpose of undertaking a hearing test. The worst that could happen in such circumstances if they were real, would be dismissal due to a medical condition; so it can be imagined how this must have frightened the living daylights out of poor Jim.

The fictitious memorandum, signed by Robert McCartney in the same turquoise coloured ink as he always used, was a master class of a forgery and the date of the appointment was set long enough forward to be after we had worked another early turn shift. Of course, he was then never late but the culprit, whose identity I never discovered, left it up until a very short time before the appointment was due, to advise him it was cancelled. His hearing problems had been miraculously healed.

Hereford City was split into 7 beats on the North Wye (City) side of the river and a few others on the other side of the river worked from the new South Wye Police Station in St. Martins Street. (Now a leisure centre and some would say that it always had been!) Each shift had one sergeant (maybe two on some occasions) to supervise them.

The briefing parade meant that we stood in a line in the parade room where we produced our appointments. I could never understand why our truncheon, handcuffs, (the old ones with accompanying screw to unlock them) whistle and pocket books were called 'Appointments'. Who, when and where were they going to meet?

Anyway, the sergeant briefed us about our duties after he had inspected our uniforms and boots and we had produced our appointments. It didn't happen that often but I can recall officers being told to go home and polish their boots, then having to work extra time at the end of their shift to make up for the time lost. When I see the body armour and the broad belts full of other equipment which is carried today, I cringe. I'm so pleased for many reasons that I didn't have to carry all that stuff and wear high visibility gear.

To be seen in public without headgear would never be known unless helmets and hats were knocked off. Neither would we be seen shopping in public. Short sleeve order in the summer was hardly ever permitted and our 'clip on' ties could never be taken off. Should the order be issued for short sleeves, then everyone had to be the same and was ordered by the divisional commander who was the only supervisor permitted to give such an order.

Of course, such things as shopping and other domestic issues could be attended to but more often than not, it was after duty when a plain jacket could be worn over the uniform.

Out of sight and out of mind. These were the benefits of actually walking the beat. We knew exactly where to get a cup of tea or a cold drink in the summer. Without actually walking the beat, these types of relationships will now, never materialise or at least, they will have been severely curtailed.

As briefly mentioned earlier, it was many years later, towards the end of my service, that the Police Federation (The staff union for officers up to Chief Inspector rank) fought for the right not to even walk into the Station until the shift start time commenced. They, of course argued, that we weren't paid for those fifteen minutes and that our attendance was purely voluntary.

My recollection was that just about everyone thought it common sense to be properly briefed and didn't mind reporting for the pre-shift briefing. How else could it be done? Most of us, if not all, were surprised that the briefing time was in our own time but how on earth were we to do the job without it? This Federation move gave the appearance of it not caring about the policing of the community, and caring only about the rights of its members. They were obviously after getting us a pay rise by being paid for those fifteen minutes but that never happened so far as I'm aware.

From that time onwards, apart from being allocated the beats to be worked, there was no time specifically allocated to record details of suspects wanted or the registration numbers of stolen vehicles or cars being used in crime. I suppose radio communication had lessened the situation to some degree. Also, officers called 'Collators' were appointed and worked to produce local intelligence sheets which contained a lot of the information we would have discussed when 'on parade'. The card index maintained by the collator was continually updated, especially by the community beat officers operating on the estates. (See RBOs later)

Well of course, briefings could be done and indeed they were done and are done today through modern technology but apart from them being less professional, it robbed us of that 'team spirit' which inevitably was created during those fifteen minutes. I guess the situation resembled something like a good football team running straight onto the pitch without a game plan as soon as they were changed into their kit; or like a surgeon performing an operation without studying the patient's medical records. It was another of those 'bricks out of the wall' and inevitably, this facilitated the lazy arriving just before the shift time and patrolling without being inspected or properly briefed. In my view, the thin edge of the wedge had been inserted.

Shift Operations

At any police station big enough to warrant around the clock shifts, varying types of shift patterns and methods of rostering them, could be found in operation and I guess that resembles a similar situation today.

Although shy as a boy, I had always liked people and chatting to them, (the nice ones of course) but directing traffic on a busy crossroads wasn't an ideal place from which to chat. This was the case on 'Two Beat' and the duty was shared between two officers alternating in half hour stints. It was necessary to wave your arms about in all weathers. You got soaking wet in the rain but the heat was probably the worst and this 'Traffic point' was exactly where the heavy lorries would often change gear billowing their exhaust fumes all over you. I'm sure the drivers did it on purpose.

This was the route taken by many cattle lorries on their way to the cattle market, a few hundred yards away and open slats on the lorries and trailers were often the cause of being sprayed with cattle urine from them as they passed.

The worst shift of all was an 8am to 4pm shift which meant that you were on this 'point duty' rotation for the whole of the eight-hour shift. It was no wonder that the 30-minute relief periods were spent in the back of the nearby Wing Hong Chinese Restaurant.

This wasn't the place to be having a chat, you were too busy dancing around, changing positions to suit the direction of traffic being directed. I do, however, remember having a brief shout to Josephine Williams who would walk past to and from the hair salon where she worked. She was my wife to be!

Very few motorists had the courage to stop for directions as they would realise that this was a crossroads on a main arterial route through the city.

139

However, I can recall two middle aged American ladies obviously in a hired car. As they drew up I was about to tell them that this wasn't the time or the place to take a photo (normally the request by Americans) when the driver said, in a strong American accent, "Officer, is this the way to 'LOGABOGOROG'? Well, that was how it sounded phonetically. With my puzzled expression, she shoved a list of destinations in my face and pointed to Loughborough. Not knowing which way you would take from Hereford, I replied, "Yes, that's it, straight on".

The shifts (Scales) of men were referred to by the letters A, B, C & D. I was on C Scale. We were split into two halves so we were either on C1 or C2. We rostered as seven straight shifts of 10pm – 6am nights, then 2pm – 10pm afternoons, then 6am – 2pm mornings.

However, the purpose of splitting the shifts into two halves was so that personnel could work other eight hour shifts in between the core hours so that more officers were deployed at times when they were needed most. For example, not all officers were required on a full night shift. From 2am in the morning, things had usually quietened down a little whereas the earlier time between 10pm until 2am could be very busy.

Therefore, when on nights, the one half of the shift would work a half night from 6pm to 2am thus increasing the number on duty between 10pm and 2am with another half of the afternoon shift who came on duty at 4pm until 12 mid-night instead of them all working 2pm to 10pm. Glancing at the below table marked in yellow, it can be seen that pub throwing out times would be covered by 3 x half shifts. The fourth shift would of course, always be on a 'Rest Day'.

A similar method was used for the early morning 6am to 2pm shift when one half of the shift would work an 8am to 4pm shift because that period between 6am and 8am was less busy.

In short, the splitting of our shifts was done for the furtherance of our policing task and not for our personal benefit. Some would prefer working the straight core shifts of 6am, 2pm and 10pm whilst others preferred the split 8am, 4pm and 6pm shifts.

EXAMPLE; - 3 shifts of 6 policemen splitting each to work six half shifts of 3 officers –

shift	6am	7	8	9	10	11	12	13	14	15	16	17	18	19	20	21	22	23	24	1	2	3	4	5
A1	A1	A1	A1	A1	A1	A1	A1	A1																
A2			A2	A2	A2	A2	A2	A2	A2	A2														
B1									B1	B1	B1	B1	B1	B1	B1	B1								
B2											B2	B2	B2	B2	B2	B2	B2	B2						
C1													C1	C1	C1	C1	C1	C1	C1	C1				
C2																	C2	C2	C2	C2	C2	C2	C2	C2

The above example shows all six half shifts and the times they worked. It indicates that between 1800 hrs. and midnight, our busiest time, when all the pubs were throwing out, fights quelled and drunks and other prisoners locked up etc., we would be able to field a third more officers from the three half shifts instead of at other times, when only 1 and 2 half shifts were deployed at times when it was much quieter.

I must have worked many other shift variations in my time but I always thought that this first system I experienced was the best. It was certainly more efficient for the job and I cringe now at the thought that the Police Federation may have eroded the efficiency that such a system produced.

It was many years later when a shift system was introduced from Ottawa, Canada which provided for more consecutive rest days to be taken, paid for by the working of longer, 12-hour shifts. That was great for the officers but if anyone had experienced, say a burglary and was unlucky enough for it to be reported the day before the officer deployed, started a shift of nights, followed by him or her taking their five consecutive rest days, you could not expect to see them for almost two weeks and it is doubtful that any enquiries would have been made into the burglary. This was not a good idea for the policing of communities but that 'Ottawa' system still exists in places today.

Communications

Our very important tool was our mouths which we were often required to utilise to get ourselves out of trouble. With no radios or other suitable means of communication in the early sixties, talking to people was often the means of learning what was going on. The chit-chat, and the rumours about the people living, working or robbing on those beats could be picked up.

How important is it these days when terrorists can be living in safe houses without their neighbours even knowing their names or where they have arrived from? Of course, it's vitally important as back in the day, the fact that someone had some new strange neighbours would most certainly have surfaced in conversation when the friendly beat bobby stopped for a chat. He would have also observed removal vans which would have pricked his curiosity. This may have been as he walked or cycled around his beat. Of course, such intelligence gathering is not made as simple when the local bobby is driving a car.

This problem was recognised quite soon after Panda cars were issued. I recall the instruction being given that we should park up our cars and have a walk around the beat. The problem with that was twofold –

1. It needed some discipline of mind to leave that comfortable warm vehicle to brave the weather. It wasn't long therefore before the instruction was hardly ever complied with.

2. The estates where this practice was important, weren't the places where one would relish leaving a police vehicle, or any other vehicle unattended for very long . Need I say more?

Patrolling the Beat

Prior to those Panda car days, being anything like a junior officer on a shift meant that almost automatically, the sergeant would post you to one of the less favoured beats. So earlier in my constable service, I could guarantee more often than not on daytime shifts, waving to the traffic on point duty and on nights, on my bike out in the suburbs of Hereford checking the factory premises on the industrial areas of the city. This wasn't always the case, of course, but the exceptions were very infrequent, or at least, they seemed to be.

The only means of communications prior to 1967 was via a 'Police Pillar' or 'Police Box'. Most of the population these days will not have seen such contraptions but had blue lights on top of them which flashed if the Police Station wanted to make contact with a beat officer.

There were only two of these pillars in Hereford and they were positioned in the main shopping centre at High Town and King Street which were on two different beats. They were obviously painted 'police blue' and were made of cast iron. Should you wish to make contact with the station, it was necessary to pull open the heavily sprung cast iron door and speak into a grid. There was no handset. With passing traffic and the hubbub of passers-by, it was therefore very difficult to hear the person on the other end of the conversation.

Its main use was for the Police Station to make contact with a foot patrol officer. If an incident happened then the blue light on top of the pillar would flash. This, of course, meant work and if you were unlucky, a member of the public would advise you that the pillar was flashing.

PC 118 D.W. Mauvan, at the King Street pillar, in the early 1950's.

I will always recall the advice I received from an older colleague – "No need to rush lad, it might be a fight, let 'em get on with it, they'll be knackered by the time we get there!"

In addition, when paraded, the sergeant would give us beat constables specific times to be at specific places. The idea was that if he wanted to speak to you, he knew where you would be at those times. These were called 'Points' or 'Meets'. Woe betides you if you did not arrive at these meets on time or if you were caught being off your beat. This literally meant that if crossing the road took you onto a different beat then you wouldn't cross that road unless an emergency occurred.

Very often the sergeant would be delayed and not meet you at a previously agreed point but you never took the chance of assuming that. If he was caught up at the station, he might cause the pillar to flash and speak to you if there was a pillar on your beat, of course. For those beats without a pillar, some points were at telephone kiosks, the numbers of which were catalogued at the Police Station. Others were outside public houses – hmm I wonder how the origin of selecting those came about? So, if it was impossible to make contact with you to be informed that the Sergeant couldn't make the meet, you would simply get on with checking your beat.

The larger police boxes (more like a small office) were located on the outskirts of the city. I can recall only three of these and they were situated far from the city centre on Resident Beat Officer territory. One was across on the south side of the river, at Saint Martins, the area in fact, where I was raised. The other two were on the Tupsley and Holmer beats. Fans of the TV show, 'Dr. Who' will recall them being named as 'Tardis' a means of space travel through time.

Similar to the Hereford Police Boxes I used in the mid 1960s.

These weren't there to provide shelter, but that was what they could do. I cannot remember windows in them but if there were, they would have been small opaque ones. There was a high wooden stool on which you could perch and a type of shelf which doubled as a desk. They were useful to write up your pocket book and to do the odd report. With stations being so far away, some would use them to eat their snack. We were obviously not supposed to hang around in them. They too had a blue light on the top and a means of communication similar to the pillars.

I recall one cold period of nights; I went into the St. Martin's Box towards the end of my shift. It was a good idea to make up your pocket book at that time so that your exit on the way home to that nice warm bed, (I should have said – BUM) wasn't delayed.

I had put my head down on my arms and woke up with a start as if the 'Tardis' were about to travel in space. I had probably been dreaming about it because it was now about 10 minutes after 6am, the time I should have reported to the sergeant as 'off duty'!

It was a very serious matter if an officer failed to show up for the end of his shift – especially 'Night Duty' as he might well be lying unconscious somewhere without any means of communicating his plight. The rest of the shift would not be able to leave because there might well be the need for a search party; in which case, the early morning shift would also be utilised.

I was going to be in deep sh**. The blue light was flashing as I exited the box and I was a couple of miles from the station and on cycle patrol and so, ignoring the blue light because I realised why it was flashing, I rode my bike as fast as I could; I doubt it had ever travelled so fast. I was wearing my cape and as I flashed down the hill immediately before the old Roman river bridge, my cape must have been flying behind me. Harry Potter would have been jealous. When at a safe distance but not too far from the station, I let one of my tyres down.

Running into the station, obviously sweating and having run out of breath, I explained that due to having a puncture, I had to push my bike all the way from St. Martins. There were suspicious looks on faces, I had gotten away with it but I never knew whether I was truly believed. There was, of course, the problem of getting my bike home as I could not inflate the tyre again until a safe distance from the station. The early turn driver of the van would have ignored me in disgust as he had been held up in putting out the 'No Waiting' cones, so in any event, the van would have been full of them anyway.

Patrolling these beats on foot certainly made officers very familiar with the territory and I remember with pride, that I could boast knowing the location of every Street, Road, Avenue, Lane or Alleyway in Hereford. I also got to know many business people and key contacts in the community. If there were no criminals to chase then what better way to pass the time than find someone to chat to and who knows, a coffee would probably appear with maybe, a snippet of information.

There was, however, one duty which, together with the mobility it came with, meant that it kept the one officer involved, in touch with our force headquarters operations room, a couple of miles out of the city, at Hafod Road, Hereford. This is probably best explained in the following chapter.

11.

IT WAS MOBILITY WOT DUN IT GUV!

Our Van – Call Sign YB15

In 1960, and probably for years prior to then, if you were not on the Traffic Division, which deployed one fast double manned patrol car on each of the three Divisions and a similar car for the newly opened Ross Spur Motorway (The M50), in 1963, then as already referenced, you walked or cycled the beat unless you were lucky enough to be so senior that you were posted to be the shift driver. Yes, apart from I think two Morris Traveller Countrymen for the CID and a similar car for the Fingerprint / Photographer Officer, there was just one police vehicle for the Division and every police officer of that day would be able to tell stories about it. I am no exception.

The vehicle was a dark blue Bedford Dormobile van / personnel carrier which initially, wasn't equipped with any police signs, sirens or a blue light, or indeed, anything which could indicate that it was a police vehicle. However, everyone living or working in the Hereford community was aware that it was 'THE' police van. The only indication of this was the VHF radio set inside, which only connected with the force operations room at our Hafod Road Headquarters, and not our Central Police Station from where we operated.

Radio transmissions were sent and received by what looked like an old-fashioned telephone handset which was holstered in a receptacle screwed to the dashboard. Its call sign was M2YB15. Although we were supposed to use this official Home Office call sign in full, we soon dropped the M2 and it simply became YB15 pronounced 'YB One Five'. The van was used for just about everything including:-

- Putting the 'No Waiting' cones out on early mornings

- Collecting Stolen Cycles and other Property

- Getting to incidents as and when required

- A Personnel Carrier (the transport) for taking staff to and from the Hereford Central Police Station to the HQ at Hafod Road

- A Black Maria (dark blue actually) for the conveyance of prisoners when they were arrested

- Conveying Prisoners to prison having been sentenced by a court

I am bound to have missed other uses but in short, it was used for every occasion when a police vehicle was required. In order to drive it, it was necessary to report to Sergeant 21 John Bourne who I think, was the only Traffic Sergeant in the force and was responsible for conducting the driving tests for officers wishing to drive this van. His other job involved the supervision of the one or two mechanics employed at the garage. So far as I was concerned, he was a very important man because it was he who would decide whether I was able to drive the van or not.

The police garage where he was based was almost next to the police station in Gaol Street and it was contained in dilapidated buildings on both sides of the road. They were more like big glorified sheds than proper garages.

On the same side of the road as the police station, was the garage which housed the roadworthy high speed 'Traffic Patrol' motor cars and within it, was a small office where the patrol car crews reported and from where John Bourne and his Police Reserve 'sidekick' Cyril Hoskins operated. It was also the place from which civilian staff and myself as a cadet, would gather and leave to be conveyed to our Hafod Road headquarters for a 9am start.

On the other side of the road was the garage where all the vehicle maintenance was conducted.

The problem was, that I hadn't that long before started to drive and apart from motorcycles, the only vehicle I had driven was our first car, a small

Austin A40 Farina. (UVJ 459) The very size of this van was enough to frighten me but when I climbed into the driver's seat, it was the first time that I consciously remembered the gear stick was missing from its normal place and was attached to the steering column. I must have seen this before but had not thought about it sufficiently for it register in my mind, until it came to driving the thing.

"Err Serge, I haven't driven with a column mounted gear lever before?"

It was as if this was an everyday occurrence for him and he replied, "No problem son, let me know when you want to change gear. You clutch and I'll change the gear".

We drove around the block with me depressing the clutch and shouting "change" and him shifting the gear stick. The whole thing lasted about five minutes; it was as if he had put the kettle on in his office and he wanted to get back to make his tea. To my amazement, I passed.

This experience in itself, amounts to another change of shape in the way we eventually went about such things because the necessary driving courses required to be completed for various types of drivers, now cost many thousands of pounds per annum, not even considering the hours lost by officers being absent from their duties.

Driving the YB15 van was, of course, the basic driving qualification requirement whereas, patrol car drivers required courses in Stafford and other places around the country; these were residential courses of some lengthy durations.

Having a good senior PC as a nominated driver of YB15 on the shift, was a benefit because as indicated above, during the very early hours of the morning, all good people should be tucked up in bed, the criminals arrested on the night would be locked up and if the sergeant had any sense, he wouldn't want to be meeting up with us at times after 3am. In short, the city was more or less asleep, and if this peace was maintained, an hour or two before we clocked off at 6am, the driver would be known to pick up those officers he could find around the beats. This patrol around the city in a warm vehicle in winter or with the doors slid back and anchored in the summer, was very welcome indeed. If you hadn't found time to stop at one of the regular coffee stops, at least you were giving your feet a rest.

The sergeant not emerging from the warmth of the station, could not, of course, be guaranteed and I recall on more than one occasion, when the alarm was sounded, and all passengers diving to the floor out of sight of the sergeant as we drove past him. The driver would need to later make some excuse to him as to why he hadn't stopped. Usually it was trying to chase some fictitious vehicle he had seen.

As mentioned earlier, every Hereford officer of that time had stories to tell about YB15. The two that have always stuck in my mind and in which I was involved, are as follows:-

1. Burcott Road on the outskirts of Hereford, (7 Beat) separated two mini–Industrial Estates. It was not only the road that separated them, a railway line also acted as a barrier. However, in order to travel from one to the other, a short cut could be taken by travelling through a pedestrian tunnel beneath the railway track. This saved quite a distance to travel and as in those days we needed to check the security of all the properties on these industrial estates, time was often critical. (Such properties are not now checked – another brick out of the wall)

The tunnel was so small however, some drivers boasted that they could drive YB15 through it. I knew this was possible because I had been driven through it myself and consequently, I was able to boast being able to do it myself. It was, after all, a tunnel of similar width to the Queen Victoria pedestrian bridge which crossed the River Wye from the King George Vth playing fields to the Castle Green near to the General hospital. This was another stupid challenge for us drivers which on reflection, could have caused us to be sacked.

It was during a reminiscent visit a few years ago, that I saw that the council had blocked vehicular passage to the bridge by the strategic placement of concrete bollards. Spoil sports!

Anyway, back to the Burcott Road tunnel, the wing mirrors needed to be pulled in to accomplish the manoeuvre. I got pretty expert at this but on nights one time as I drove into the tunnel, all of the vehicle's lights were extinguished. I reversed out and to my delight, the lights came back on again. I alighted and to my horror, I had forgotten that this was the first shift I had used the van after it had been fitted with a blue light.

When I started the shift, I sneakily put it on to see it flash a few times but I couldn't wait to be sent to an emergency so that I could show it off as I drove through Hereford. It was necessary to literally crawl through the tunnel and hence the light wasn't smashed or severely damaged. I found it slightly bent off centre so when it was pushed back again to the upright position, it didn't look damaged at all, and above all, it worked. So that's all right then? – no problem, or so I thought.

I should say here, that if anything happened on your beat on night duty, for example, a burglary that you hadn't discovered or anything else that required clarification, then as a matter of course, you would be rudely woken and questioned about it. I was so conscious of this that I can recall that when I had been busy with a prisoner and with the accompanying administration, on my way home after booking off duty, I would check the parts of my beat that I had failed to check during my tour of duty. This was simply driving around and shining my torch to make sure that windows or doors weren't obviously damaged. It was not just me who would do that; it was standard practice by most; a work ethic or an attitude of mind to have completed the job! Another brick kicked out of that wall?

Anyway, my doorbell rang that following day and, I was woken and questioned about not reporting damage to YB15. The best thing to do was to admit the problem and accept the rollicking which sure enough followed!

2. Hereford Rugby Club was then situated at Rockfield Road, (an aptly named rough lane) at the bottom of Aylestone Hill, as Hereford is entered from the Worcester direction. The pitch was bounded by this lane leading to the club house and on its far side by the main railway line. As the ground rose from that railway line, houses in the distance on Bodenham Road ran parallel to it and overlooked the rugby pitch. Being so close to the railway embankment meant that the pitch was full of wild rabbits during the night time as their burrows were made in the banks carrying the railway.

In those early hours, if time permitted, now and again, we found it good fun to drive onto the rugby pitch and try to mesmerise the rabbits in the headlights. With both front side doors slid back and secured with the strap provided, we could creep up on the rabbits and by throwing our truncheons at them, try to hit them darting all over the rugby pitch. I might say now, that I never knew of one being hit but it was good fun trying.

It was on one such occasion, Sergeant 23 Gerry Surrell was the sergeant on duty in the Information Room at Hafod Road and PC George Matthews was his constable partner. These were the only two employed in the information room and having been an Inspector in the force's Operations Room in 1973, I now smile when I consider the number of staff then employed. There must have been 20-30 staff on each shift but back in the Hereford day, just one sergeant and one constable. Civilian staff were never even dreamt of.

I could write a book about Gerry and George but perhaps another day. George was an ex-Grenadier Guardsman and Gerry Surrell made more money from his smallholding than he did in the police.

Suffice to say here, that as we were tearing around trying to dispatch these rabbits, the radio broke its silence. It was Sergeant Surrell in his gruff voice shouting our call sign – "YB15, YB15, are you receiving – over"?

I sort of sighed to myself because it wasn't unusual for Gerry to say, "Another five please". This was a code for us to buy a packet of five Players Weights cigarettes for him as he had run out. Not ten or twenty, but you could buy five in those days. My everlasting memory of these occasions was trying to get the money off him when we delivered. Out would come a leather 'flip open' type of purse. The top would lift open to reveal the back of the lid and change could be shaken onto it from the bottom where the coin would be prevented from dropping to the ground by a lip built onto the top. It was as if the crown jewels were inside this purse. He would rattle it around and if you were lucky, the correct amount of change would be found for the painful act of handing it over.

Of course, on this occasion it was in the early hours and so it couldn't have been for cigarette shopping.

I responded to his call

"Yes, YB15 here Sarge, receiving – over"

"Good, - YB15, what's your location? – over"

I was hardly going to say that we were chasing rabbits on the rugby pitch and so, as the Railway Station was on the other side of the main road I replied:-

"We're at Railway Station approach Serge – over".

His reply was – "Just the right bloody place, nip over to the rugby ground will you, there's some bloody idiot driving a van around on the pitch!"

Hmmn......Rockfield Road was a cul-de-sac so I left it for a minute or so and then had to sadly report that the van must have nipped out of Rockfield Road before we had a chance to get over there........

Although I had no part in it, I had been told of a similar occasion when another driver, chasing a rabbit, continued the chase out of Rockfield Road a good distance into the High Town. The passenger threw his truncheon at it and as it missed, it skidded off the road surface and cracked a very large window belonging to one of the stores in High Town.

I hesitate to mention the name of the shop – 'Greenlands', in case any of the directors are alive today and who might attempt making a claim! It 'wasn't me guv' anyway but the General Occurrence Book (GOB) later contained a brilliantly recorded report about how a passing lorry must have thrown up a stone to have caused the damage.

I'm now realising that as I had suspected, I've fallen into the trap of wittering on forever about these stories. I always intended to make the book light and humorous but without taking over the script of the main story. However, they have served to remind me how the policing of those days was performed.

Suffice it to say that in my view, people and property were protected far more diligently and efficiently in those days and although we were always lacking in personnel and resources, we obviously had more time. This is a clear indication that our paymasters have not kept up with the times in securing these resources.

It was intended that the property checks made on night duty were completed once before refreshment breaks and again, afterwards. Every door of every shop or office premises was tried. A constable would have patrolled every street, road, avenue lane or alleyway in the urban beats. As indicated above, the premises listed in the vacant premises register, also had a good chance of a visit. One cannot argue that this latter duty would not be regarded as a police duty in more modern times, however, it fell within the definition of a Constable and it was achieved whenever possible, at least once during every tour of night duty.

I hesitate to mention that every property being checked, also included the Cathedral where valuables such as the chain library and Mappa Mundi were kept.

As an Ex-Cadet, I was aware of, but spared the experience. It appears that gaining entry into the Cathedral on nights was something of a tradition which went back to when the officer on three beat was expected to stoke

154

up the boilers with coke. It was hardly the place you would want to shelter or have a warm though.

As also apparently happened at Worcester, the key to the door was kept for this purpose at the police station. Parent Constables would show recruits the procedure but unbeknown to the recruit, another constable would have been let in before him armed with a white sheet..... Need I say more?

I can verify that entering the Cathedral in the middle of the night armed with just a torch for light is very unnerving at the best of times but when something looking like a white ghost appears from behind a concrete pillar uttering the strangest of sounds; it's a miracle that there were no heart attacks occurring.

On nights at Hereford, we were blessed with two window cleaners, Horace and Eric. They worked as partners and so far as I can recall, they were the only two window cleaners who operated in the City Centre. It was therefore necessary for them to start at about 4am and their first port of call was the Police Station so that they could fill their buckets with hot water. Thinking back, they were very honoured to be able to do that because relationships with 'civilians' wasn't that frequent then and to the extent of being allowed free access into the inner sanctum of the Police Station, especially to fill buckets up with hot water.

In order to carry their ladders they had made what looked like a large wooden box about three feet long. On each side they had fixed one bicycle wheel, so that when they let it go, the box would rock down and prop up at an angle. The purpose of the box was so that they could transport their ladders around the town as they worked. If a ladder lay across the top of the box then if they then let go of it, the one end of the ladder would prop the box up. In other words, the mobile box became a fulcrum for transporting the ladders.

Anyway, how they put up with us I'll never understand. In fact Horace would always get himself wound up because one of the 'Bobbies' would pinch the cart when they were both at the top of their individual ladders. I think it was Archie Buttriss, our Welsh National Shot-Put Champion who was also known to bring out the 'white sheet' and play similar tricks on them.

So, returning to my theme about police mobility and coverage, it soon became apparent that with just this one van, YB15, covering for out-of-town areas, that became almost impossible without further wheels. The van would invariably be engaged on other matters as in addition to the uses listed earlier, it was sometimes required to make out of town enquiries and the recording of witness statements etc.

I recall receiving one of those big bollockings one never forgets. Henry Wiggin Ltd was probably the largest employer in Hereford at the time and one of its executive's sons had been left in charge of the very smart and expensive house at Holmer, whilst his parents were on holiday. This son foolishly decided to hold a party in their absence and in short it got out of hand, was gate crashed and numerous valuable articles were stolen.

I had been given the crime to investigate and was fortunate enough to have eventually recovered most of the property and detected many who were responsible. I needed to record a simple witness statement from someone about the recovery of some property but my mistake was the obtaining of this statement, whilst I had use of the van, on a Friday night on night duty. Of course the van was needed for other emergencies, especially on a Friday night and whilst recording the statement, I was off the air with the radio.

It was Sergeant 100 Neville Ovens who later retired as the Chief Constable of Cheshire, who handed out my much-deserved bollocking. He had been one of our star officers selected to be on the 'Special Course' who was identified as one of our future Chief Constables. We remained friends of course, and I know he and Jean reside not too far away at Ross on Wye, where Neville is a member of the Ross Golf Club. I was grateful when, in

2017, he agreed to give the final toast to the memory of the Herefordshire Constabulary which, 50 years earlier had been swallowed up through the amalgamation which formed the West Mercia Constabulary.

So, this story has helped me to describe the problems of having just this one van to carry out all of these duties. We were lucky to be able to have use of it but for the main we remained unlucky in having to 'plod' around our beats. Trips to the chiropodist would then definitely be out of our reach!

Unit Beat Policing (Panda Cars)

We were one of the first police forces to embrace what was known then as 'Unit Beat Policing'. Not only were some lucky ones going to get to drive these vehicles but in addition, we were going to be able to talk to the police station and even our fellow colleagues whether in cars or on foot. One can imagine how useful this would be. By golly, this was most definitely the beginning of a huge change of shape for and a new chapter in the history of policing.

How pleased we all were when, in 1967, small saloon cars of every description came onto the scene so that our policing tasks could be achieved with greater speed and efficiency. In Herefordshire, they were Ford Anglia models as depicted below, but elsewhere varying makes and models were used.

We were additionally issued with hand held Pye radios. In fact there were two parts to each radio set. The transmitting part had a 'pop up' radio aerial which 'popped up' whenever the transmission button was pressed to talk. The other half was to listen to the messages received. So one wasn't much use without the other.

In addition, this was the year when also, the breathalyser was introduced and so the little plastic green boxes containing the breathalyser equipment were carried in these cars. These panda cars were in effect, mobile police stations and in quieter times, one could sit in them to write up pocket books and reports. This happened to change the whole concept of how we were to carry out those duties as defined above, in order to protect our communities. It was a massive change and sadly, unless you were on a city centre beat on nights, the shaking hands with door knobs was a thing of the past.

I recall stopping in a layby to make up my pocket book for it to be signed off at the end of my night duty. I hadn't intended to drop off to sleep but I had, for just a few seconds. All of a sudden I was woken by the noise and two headlights of a lorry coming straight for me. It was like being in a nightmare but it wasn't; my foot jammed onto the brake pedal and I wrestled with the steering wheel. Phew, it was just for a second or two that I had forgotten that I was stationary in the layby parallel to the road, but it didn't half frighten me.

One of the first Panda Cars to be used – PC 178 'Docker' Main at the wheel

The inception of this scheme was to be on 1st August 1967, just short of our amalgamation. I was a young upcoming PC who had been selected, quite young in service, to become a 'Parent Constable' to show new recruits around and bed them down into their duties and procedures.

There's no way that I can 'dress up' walking the beats for eight hours with only one official refreshment break of 45 minutes. If, for nothing else, whilst it was enjoyable mixing with the community, it was hard work on the feet and the legs, so what a pleasure it was, for these cars to be issued to us. Since 1829, policing had been worked on the beat and the beats were patrolled on foot. We couldn't believe what had happened, what a great time to be involved in this historic changing of the shape of our organisation. This new system was a fine concept which, if adequately resourced, had the hallmarks of being a brilliant scheme.

It was a coincidence that we were on 2pm x 10pm shift when they were actually presented to the press and I was one of three drivers of the very first of them. I had better explain in more detail how the system worked.

There were variations across the country, but basically in Hereford, one Panda Car would form an area of patrol which equated to two or three of the Resident Beat Officer (RBO) beats, however, there were many occasions when not all RBO houses were filled even when they were, officers were absent due to sick leave or being required to take their leave and rest days. This situation meant that without them, very often the only patrol available on the area was the 'Panda Car'. Put in the police vernacular, they were running around like 'blue arsed flies'.

In theory, any enquiry picked up by a Panda Car driver, should have been handed over to the RBO to take over when he or she returned to duty. This wasn't always convenient and in any case, the last thing wanted was for these Panda car drivers to be bogged down with the administration which was always intended to be done by the RBOs, so that the drivers were free to be a first response to other incidents.

The Death of Rural Policing.

The results were inevitable. It became a lot easier and convenient to direct a mobile officer to a scene than to hang about for an RBO. With all this mobility and excellent communications, was there now a need to employ

RBOs and Village bobbies if a car could be despatched to their areas in double quick time?

In addition, with such rapid communications and mobility, why were Police Authorities and the taxpayers living in these areas, being required to pay for the upkeep of all these police accommodations? The value of the police properties owned represented huge capital sums of money. Without a full establishment of officers, county forces such as Herefordshire could not be organised in such a way to facilitate the proper working of these Unit Beats as described. Although the changes were greeted with enthusiasm, because of these shortages, the concept never really took off as it was planned to be and it wasn't long before the public were asking for more bobbies to be put back on the beat. The term 'Fire Brigade policing' had already emerged in the press.

It seemed as though bobbies had been removed from their villages and estates at a stroke! No one was thrown out of their police accommodation but inevitably, many of the officers applied to purchase the police houses and old police stations they then occupied and when others became vacant, they were sold on the open market. Why pay to maintain what you weren't using, the revenue received could be used in other spheres of policing? In my view this was a drastic action and I distinctly remember saying to myself that this was tantamount to selling off the family silver. Being at the centre of any community, being as that maybe in the city, on estates or in rural villages, was the core to our policing initiative.

It wasn't long before villages lost their police officer forever and bobbies walking the beat would become rarities. With their colleagues rushing around in cars, the style of policing saw the end of the 'Panda Car' as it was then known and improvements were made by the introduction of 'Sub Divisional Response Cars' (SDRVs). These were saloon cars of a slightly higher specification, and the shape of our policing had changed again. In addition, later firearms incidents which required a fast police firearms team response were attended by use of these vehicles, the drivers of which were required to be skilled drivers in addition to being firearms trained. I had never before even seen a police firearm although I was aware that a few officers were trained in their use. John Joseph of Ross on Wye, I believe was one of the first. RIP John.

In retrospect, these changing shapes occurred fairly rapidly in comparison to changes in other eras of policing. The resultant changes and their effects, never really hit me until I was able to view them all in retrospect, much like the primitive versions of the cinema where the 'Flicks' which consisted of numerous images on cards quickly flicked and viewed, portrayed the full story quite effectively, as opposed to examining one card individually at a time.

This selling off of our 'family silver' was like an analogy of trying to stop a giant tanker. The sequence of events was so rapid and now without those village police stations and residential beats, nothing could stop that tanker even by slamming on the brakes.

It was now far too late. It makes me so sad to believe that any 'halfway' house couldn't have worked. Instead, we were made to suffer a slow decline in their numbers. On top of all that, despite the general cry to put more bobbies on the beat, the then Home Secretary Theresa May, later cut the establishment of English and Welsh Police forces by 20,000. What crazy idea was behind that?

It can only be assumed that this was at a time when she had, some would say, no good cause to fall out with the Police Union, the Police Federation of England and Wales which serves police officers up to and including the Chief Inspector rank, for it came at a time when spiralling drugs misuse and its associated social problems were becoming uncontrollable.

That action was indefensible and we continue to struggle to replace them under a different administration. But the consequences will be synonymous to treading water because those that left were experienced and the slow recruitment process to replace them, will consist of raw recruits who will need to be trained and gain the past experiences which have been lost.

In my view, the damage caused by the removal of local bobbies cannot be overemphasised. The police officers patrolling these estates and villages, got to know the residents they policed. As well as knowing all the villains and who, among them, were committing the crimes; they would know who to go to for information. I'm not referring to paid informants here, these would be good upright citizens who wanted to retain the peace and well-being of their communities as well as their police officers. This local intelligence was suddenly missing. Who knows who is living next door to whom these days? As mentioned earlier, with the spread and increase of terrorism, how important would that be today?

I've no doubt that some crimes recorded in rural areas were viewed as not worthwhile being investigated. They may well have been 'cuffed', the vernacular for not recording them. This would also help with detection rates. Even if the crime statistics in those rural areas were analysed today, after such a long period of time, I dare say hardly any crimes at all would be recorded. But why?

I contend the answer to be, because there's no police there to receive them and the local populace know only too well that it would be a waste of their time to ring the main police stations in the towns and cities to report them. It appears that the only encouragement to report crimes has evolved from insurance companies insisting on a crime report reference being available. Let me refer to my work in the countryside where some examples how contact with the village communities was appreciated:-

Alfrick a Section in 'The Sticks'.

When performing my rural sergeant duties at Alfrick, one wouldn't be surprised to know that at Christmas time, a bottle, or a brace of pheasants or even a chicken might well come the way of my beat officers and occasionally, to myself. Such gifts would not have been accepted had receivers thought for one second that any ulterior motive was involved. Here are some examples: -

The Sergeants house at Alfrick was next door to the Constable's house and was separated by a small office in the centre which was accessible to both houses through inner doors. The public obviously called at the front office door.

As the Sergeant, I was responsible for the supervision of many of the village stations on the sub division but being resident in one village, it just wasn't worth explaining to residents of Alfrick that they didn't really have a sergeant and a constable to look after them exclusively. However this being the position, when the Alfrick constable was on leave or taking his rest days, and with me wanting to keep my hand in, especially when suspects were available to be questioned, I never turned any contact away or pushed jobs onto others.

I recall over one period of time, one of the village publicans had done a 'moonlight flit' and the office telephone was hot with callers asking me where the landlord had scarpered to, owing them all various sums of money. These debts were not, of course, criminal matters because they were civil debts. However, the post office being run by a Mrs Boucher wasn't too far away from the pub and I was getting so much hassle with the phone calls, I knew she might well know some answers.

She was a lovely lady who always insisted on providing a cup of tea and a lovely slice of fruit cake to go with it. By the way, would this be regarded as accepting a gift and therefore contrary to regulations? Technically it did but

I don't quote this for that reason and, of course I would enjoy it anyway. I mentioned to her what had happened and eventually asked her directly, "Do you have any idea where they have gone to Mrs B"? She stroked her chin for a while before telling me that she hadn't. Then she said, "But Serge, would you like the registration number of the removal van?"

I could have kissed her. Let's just say that things worked out well. No, not even a police matter, but how well it describes the worthiness of police and community relationships. I could never see that sort of information being accessible to the police these days without there being some sort of relationship with the village population and its police officers.

On another occasion, as the Alfrick constable was off duty, I used his panda car to travel across to visit another beat officer stationed in the village of Broadwas when a pheasant flew out of the hedge directly in front of me. The collision left me with a small but very noticeable dent in the front bonnet of the car before it flew into the air, landing in the field belonging to a farmer who happened to be the husband of one of the magistrates I often stood before, whilst prosecuting in the Worcester County Magistrates' court. (A duty performed when the Inspector was absent)

The field gate was nearby and I entered the field to retrieve the freshly killed pheasant. My intention was to bag it and that we'd have roasted pheasant for Sunday's dinner. The bird having landed in the field was technically the property of the owner and so, as soon as I returned to the car again I thought to myself that it would just be my luck that someone saw me put it into the panda car. So, I thought that if I offered the bird to the farmer, he was bound to give it to me anyway.

I banged on the farmhouse door with pheasant in hand and as he opened it I said, "Oh good afternoon I hit this and it landed in your field and so as technically it's yours, I thought I'd deliver it for you before the flies pitched on it".

He took it off me and said, "Thanks Sarge, I'll boil it up for the dogs!" Well, that didn't work out as I had thought but my conscience was clear. It was this same farmer and his wife who owned a section of the nearby river Teme on their land which was fished by a Birmingham Angling Society. It was tradition that she would always be presented with the first salmon caught in the season and similarly, she would donate it to the local pub at Lulsley, the Fox and Hound. The Scots publican, Mr and Mrs Jock Brown would cook it in a proper fish kettle to be eaten at a social occasion put on ostensibly for the Alfrick and Lulsley Fisherman's Club.

The problem was that I never investigated this club fully enough to be actually convinced that such a club existed. However, she always managed to be sat on the bench when an application was heard for an extension of licensing hours for this pub in order that this 'first salmon' could be toasted and consumed by all who attended the social evening.

I'm not sure how it came about but it also always seemed to be when the Inspector was absent and I was called to take his place in court that these applications were made. No objections to the licensing extensions applied for, were ever made. I was quite happy that this sort of thing hadn't been in mind when legislators were drawing up statutes to prevent police officers being used or pressured into currying favour.

It was embarrassing at one Christmas time when waiting for the magistrates to emerge from their retiring room into the court. The Clerk to the magistrates, Harry Hazlewood and I had already had a glass of sherry with the justices before they emerged. I had also already received some carrier bags with pheasant tails protruding from them from licensees who were there waiting to hear their applications for extensions to their licensing hours for special occasions. The bags were down by the chair on which I sat.

John Barker, the Licensee from the Swan Inn at Alfrick had arrived late when I recall hearing the 'clink, clink clink' of bottles striking each other in time with the steps being taken from whoever it was, carrying the bag. "Have a good Christmas Sarge" John whispered in my ear. The justices were bound to have heard the clinking of the bottles and his whispered message to me but they would have known too, that such gifts were made in good faith and would not have caused me to carry out my duties otherwise than in the way I should have done.

Whilst I fully believe that such actions weren't unethical, I was fully aware of the caution required to ensure that the thin edge of such a wedge wasn't being inserted. I knew that such incidents were petty in the extreme compared with the huge 'bungs' and organised crimes alleged to have involved police officers in metropolitan areas. I was pretty sure that the petty incidents described here, would never be regarded as discreditable conduct.

To repeat my conclusions however, the relaxing of the restrictions to private lives could have been made much sooner. Now that village police stations and resident beat houses were no longer occupied, Chief Officers would not normally be forcing officers to be posted to these outstations as they used to. I guess that also, with an ounce of common sense being thrown in, it finally reflected that we were living in more enlightened times.

12.

PROCESSING THE LAW IN CRIME DETECTION

To repeat what I've said before, it matters not whether the changes I have discussed in this book appeared in my earlier years of policing or not. In such examples, one needs to refer to very early practices in order to comment on changes which may have occurred far later in my service. It was the playing of the game, 'Cops and Robbers' is what I enjoyed as a boy and I think I brought that enjoyment into my professional life in the police service.

This was experienced more so in the early parts of my service and much later on when serving as a Detective Chief Inspector in two divisions and later as a Detective Superintendent, deputy to the head of the Force CID for about a year. Those days however, were when catching criminals was the name of the game as opposed to sitting at my desk facing a pile of paperwork. As a young constable, with less than three years' service, I was lucky to have received a period as an 'Aide to CID' at Hereford.

Such attachments were viewed as types of apprenticeships for those uniformed bobbies who showed an aptitude for CID work. Whilst there was little chance of getting into CID with my young service, it was excellent training and a worthwhile experience. I was particularly in awe at the interviewing skills displayed by the two Detective Sergeants, the long-deceased Ken Lawley and Phil Paton. They knew who was committing the crime in Hereford and worked tirelessly to obtain confessions when those individuals were arrested.

In those days, there were no restrictions such as are now documented within the provisions of the 'Police and Criminal Evidence Act of 1984'. (PACE) There was, a genuine desire to catch criminals and when caught, to extract as many confessions out of them as possible. It was not unusual to arrest suspects on a Friday afternoon and if they did not confess, to leave them in the cells all over the weekend to resume 'talks' on Monday morning.

It must be remembered that PACE was years away and no-one had heard of 'Custody Sergeants'. Whilst evidence gathering would normally continue throughout those weekends, the prisoners were fed and otherwise looked after by the Station Duty Officer who also had a hundred and one other things to do, including roasting our meal on nights. All visits to them were recorded on the rear of charge sheets and the need to do this frequently, was a reminder that they were in custody.

This sort of situation was, of course, abused though I hasten to add not to any unfair or serious extent in Herefordshire, so far as I was aware. Abuse of powers inevitably led to the 'PACE' Act which, in effect, tied policemen's hands behind their backs. Funny when I reminisce now, we had in mind the victims; well, probably those who had offended against the victims. Protecting the guilty, which seems to be the main objective today, was furthest from our minds.

We did not thank those before us whose actions led us down this path but at the same time, we were detecting crime and never ever realised that this would, in effect, be obstructed by this legislation.

I saw the transition in motion when we emerged from those days into the restrictions imposed by the Codes of Practice of PACE. I was then in the Chief Superintendent rank which meant that I had been drawn away from being a practitioner in the field of capturing suspects and drawing confessions of guilt from them. I was, however. to take part in the effects of PACE by being called to Police Stations to authorise the continued custody of prisoners, if that was what was required.

I could sense that this had knocked the stuffing out of investigating officers who were enthusiastically keen to clear up more undetected crimes than their mates did on the previous shift. As necessary as the changes were perceived to be, it became a huge hammer with disastrous consequences in the art of catching criminals and preventing crime. I shall refer to this later at a more appropriate time.

The name of the game was to cultivate informants and at Hereford I struck up a relationship with a man called Stanley RUCK. Stan was a bit of a 'dosser' or 'sleeper out' who I had already chatted up and realised that he had come from better stock than that. He occasionally worked as a cattle drover in the Cattle Market but kept himself clean, loved cider and above all he was a good burglar. Stan was never going to get enrolled into a Hatton Garden jewel heist but you see, his 'bottom of the league' burglaries were recorded as a crime, just the same as the Brinks Matt burglary, so in Herefordshire, having one burglary committed and one burglary detected represented a 100% detection rate. It's good to dream!

Unfortunately for Stan, he was so good that his modus operandi was in effect the 'Hallmark' of his trade and so, was easily recognisable.

He would select a window to be broken and near its handle would strike the window with the end of a pole, like the handle of a broom with such velocity, much like that of a bullet. This caused the window not to smash and fall to the ground in many pieces causing a commotion, but to pierce a fine circular hole, not much wider than the diameter of the stick. He would then lever up the handle to open the window.

Such a burglary was reported one day at The Railwayman's Canteen on the Railway Station approach. Would you believe, it was just that, a canteen for railwaymen! Some food had been stolen, gammon, cheese and such like also razor blades, tobacco and cigarette papers and many more items which although didn't amount to much was just the type of property sought by the likes of Stan Ruck or other of his 'dosser' mates. With the 'Modus Operandi' as described above, the culprit had to be Stan.

I put the word out around town and his usual haunt around the bus station, that I was looking for him and although he was unusually more difficult to locate, we eventually met. To cut a long story short I locked him up to stew for a while to interview him later after briefly being told that "It wasn't me Guv".

As expected, Stan denied all knowledge of the burglary and during my interview with him, by sheer coincidence, the head of the CID of the day, Detective Inspector Charles (Charlie) Lappage paid an unexpected visit from his office at Hafod Road. Charlie had replaced Dai Davies as the Detective Inspector when Dai retired and until then, I hadn't realised that he had been a Hereford detective. He joined me but between us we could not extract a confession. Mr. Lappage was a real gentleman whose appearance was nothing like a detective. He wore a bowler hat and carried a cane. He had an unusually posh accent for a Hereford chap and this was quite a novelty because he had come up through the ranks like all others, to head the force's CID.

To my utter surprise, he marched Stan into the Charge Room and told him in no uncertain terms that he was very lucky that we needed his cell for a while and that he was being bailed to return to the police station later that night. I think it would be about 10.30pm that he was supposed to return. (After the pubs had shut) I couldn't believe that he was just going to let him go for the evening, whilst still in custody in the hope that he would return.

I stood back and was just a spectator and although I was just an inexperienced sprog, I knew that papers were required to be prepared and signed before anyone could be released on police bail. There was no mention of the interview or his bailment recorded in the charge book as there should have been. If anyone had then examined it, they would have been under the impression that Stan was still in custody. None of this administration was completed and off went Stan promising to return later on. I didn't see it, but others in the office later mentioned that they wouldn't have put it past Charlie to have given Stan five bob to ensure that he got some cider down him.

I was dumbfounded until Charlie Lappage explained that he knew Stan inside out. He said that he would go straight down to the Commercial hotel, have a few pints of cider and he bet me that he would return at the appointed time and confess his crime. If I had had any money in my pocket, I would have bet to the contrary.

Needless to say, I was at the Police Station waiting for Stan to unexpectedly, so far as I was concerned, arrive. Amazingly, there he was at the front counter. He had obviously had a drink and after he had used the toilet, I sat him down and after a few questions he volunteered to take me to where he had stashed his loot. This wasn't far from the Railwayman's Canteen he had burgled. He crawled into a culvert which ran beneath Station Approach and that was where he recovered the stolen property. I bet I was just as happy (and surprised) as those detectives in London who, in later years had arrested the 'Brinks Matt' burglars for their £26 million burglary.

On a later occasion when I had occasion to arrest Stan, I paraded him in front of the sergeant in the charge room so that I could explain his arrest and to record the details of him and the charge, in the charge book. The sergeant asked Stan for his address. We both expected him to say, 'No Fixed Abode' when out of the blue he replied, "1 Barrack Square, Gloucester" I was surprised to say the least and exclaimed, "who lives there then Stan"? He replied, *"I don't know all their names but I suppose I'm going to be there for the next six months, so I'll have plenty of time to find out who's there"*. The penny dropped and I realised that this was the address of Gloucester prison.

Jumping the gun to a time not too long after our marriage, we were in our flat above a grocer's shop in Hinton Road, Hereford and whilst staring out of the window, there I saw Stan walking up from the river footpath. I quickly told Jo that he was my informant and as I dashed down the stairs the last thing I heard from her was, "Don't bring him in here".

To cut another longer story short, I ended up with some promises of information from him for which I paid with the very suit that I wore at our marriage.

So, my enjoyment at detecting crime was now fuelled by my period as a CID aide. I became even keener and had retained that interest in clearing up crime, for the rest of my active service in no matter what rank I held.

Not many weeks had passed by, when stood on duty in High Town by the police pillar, I saw Stan's mate, I think his name was Archie Bright, walking towards me wearing 'MY WEDDING SUIT'. Stan had obviously sold it for cider money and I can't recall ever getting any more information from him either. Whilst Stan was about my size, Archie Bright was a couple of feet shorter and if it was Archie, he would have had to have half of the legs of the trousers cut off!

My Aide to CID period culminated in me getting a fair report from Phil Paton which, in polite terms, suggested that I was a little green behind the ears; and that I could do with more experience before I would be considered for a CID post. After all, I had not yet completed three years' service, there was plenty of time ahead of me.

It's sad to record here that 44 years later, I attended Phil Paton's Funeral at Fownhope, Herefordshire. He had been and had remained, the best Interviewer of suspects I had ever had the privilege to witness. He would have no need to beat the desk and behave like a bad cop. It was the way he asked the questions and the skill and variable speed in which he applied in phrasing them.

I attended his funeral with others, Chris Furber and Barrie Pearce, two of my current mates who meet monthly for lunch and who had been in the CID as Detective Constables sometime after I had left Hereford on promotion.

We were about to leave the wake but were asked by one of Phil's children to hang fire so that we could talk about some of their father's skills, especially his interviewing skills. She had overheard us reminiscing and so the rest of the family present were keen to be involved in the conversation when most of the others had left the wake.

Fate and a lot of luck had dictated that I was able to gain promotion, in my view, (and others) way before my time and it was this, which robbed me of the experience I could have received as a Detective Constable. I knew however, that for the long-term benefit of my family, I was better off on the ladder of promotion.

The Disclosure of Evidence

But oh, how things have changed.

It must be said that in my early days of catching criminals, in no way would it even be contemplated that we would prejudice our own cases against defendants, by showing our hand with any evidence which would be harmful to our case. That is not to say, of course, that not to divulge such things, would be part of a conspiracy to falsely convict them. Such an idea was anathema to what we wanted to achieve, which simply was to lock up those who had contravened the law, not to detect crimes by falsely accusing others who may not have been responsible.

Phil Paton and Ken Lawley, my old Detective Sergeants would have been spinning in their graves if they were made aware of how the emerging rules of 'Disclosure' and the effects of the 'PACE' Act had contributed to the lack of interest now emerging in the rank-and-file equivalent of the old 'thief catchers' of the past and those who were to follow them. The pendulum had swung far too far in favour of those suspected of committing crimes and to hell with the victims or those trying to catch them.

Practice and procedures decided by higher courts have since dictated that not to disclose evidence helpful to the defence is **'UNFAIR TO THE DEFENDANT'** This is what the rules on disclosure are all about, and why they are so important, because those acting for the defence, need not only to be served with evidential material which is relied upon to convict, but they now have to be informed of any material which may go towards helping their defence. They are also informed of any material that the prosecution term as 'unused' which they receive as schedules and are open to inspection.

I have placed the 'unfair to the defendant' quote above in upper case and in bold type because, whilst unfairness and trickery may not be tolerated, I need to ask the question, are similar rules set to ensure **fairness to their victims and also, is such a duty placed on the defence?**

'Disclosure' began to hit the headlines in notorious cases, just prior to my retirement. Bearing in mind that my retirement was in November 1994, the first major piece of legislation covering the subject was The Criminal Procedure and Investigations Act 1996. (CPIA) Its various parts and its Codes of Practice provide additional guidance which basically, deal with all aspects of evidence to be used or not to be used (unused material) in criminal proceedings.

Without wanting to turn this into a tutorial, the rules apply to: -

1. an officer in charge (OIC) of the investigation (responsible for directing the investigation and ensuring there are proper procedures for recording information and keeping records);
2. a disclosure officer (responsible for examining retained material, revealing it to the prosecutor and revealing material to the defence at the prosecutor's request)
3. a prosecutor (responsible for conducting the prosecution itself).

One such case which became notorious to the nation and which resulted in a conviction being quashed was that of the murder of the pregnant Worcester lady, Marie Wilks which occurred on the M50 Motorway on 18th June 1988. She had broken down and was attempting to use the emergency telephone at the side of the motorway.

Subsequently a man from Wales by the name of Eddie Browning as shown in the below photograph, was adjudged to have been wrongly convicted of the murder.

Browning had been sentenced to life in prison. In May 1991 his conviction and sentence were upheld on appeal. It was later discovered that the police concealed such exculpatory evidence from Browning's legal team that the murderer's car was different from Browning's car. Browning filed a new appeal against conviction, and on May 14, 1994 the Court of Appeal quashed his conviction. The charge was dismissed and he was released after six years of so called 'wrongful' imprisonment. In the year 2000, Browning filed a claim for compensation, and he was awarded £675,000.

Eddie Browning showing his almost white 'flat & floppy' hair

I took no part in the investigation but I was the officer who conducted the identification parades held at Redditch Police Station during the investigation. I was also the officer, who following his release, was directed to examine the papers so that I could present a case against a Detective Chief Inspector (then a Superintendent) in a Disciplinary Tribunal as directed by the Police Complaints Authority (PCA) who were obviously wishing to appease the public who, I suppose were baying for blood as to why this travesty of justice had happened.

This was a bizarre situation because when this course of action was imparted by the PCA to the Chief Constable, David Blakey, who, in company with two members of the PCA, would normally sit as the Chairman of the tribunal, he replied to them that the Investigating Officer and his deputy had since retired from the force and that the DCI, now the subject of their concern, was down the list of seniority to such an extent, that it would be unfair to have him appear before him as the negligent officer.

I never received the papers concerning exactly what this so-called withheld evidence was all about, as obviously details of it weren't included in the papers I had initially received. I later learned that an off-duty police officer witness had allegedly driven past the scene at the time of the murder. He had been sent to be hypnotised in an effort to recall the registration number of a vehicle believed to be owned by the assailant and which was parked close to the scene of the abduction or the murder.

When this witness was subsequently interviewed by the Senior Investigating Officer following his hypnosis, he suggested that he was not properly hypnotised and that he couldn't recall the registration number anyway. However, when pressed, he said that he had described a number but impressed upon the officers that it was given, just to satisfy those trying to hypnotise him and that he was not confident at all, that this was the number in question and would not also be confident that his evidence should be used. It appears that this was the evidence which was to release Browning because the description of the number given by the so-called hypnotised witness, turned out to be nothing like Browning's registration number.

In effect, Mr Blakey was telling the PCA that this officer was not to blame and as a result, they responded by disqualifying him from chairing the tribunal as he had already disclosed his verdict. Instead, they appointed Sir Keith Povey who was then, the Chief Constable of Leicestershire and later, Her Majesty's Chief Inspector of Constabulary.

One cannot say that Browning had escaped Scott-free, because officially, he had been declared as wrongfully convicted. I feel safe, however, in stating that there was little doubt (nay no doubt whatsoever) among the officers who had a better understanding of the evidence than myself, that he was nothing but responsible for Marie's death.

In addition, I have mentioned my peripheral involvement in being the identification parade officer, because of the concern I felt as to what happened on it. As can be seen in his photographs above, Browning's hair was blonde and very thin and floppy, it was flat down on his head. When he was brought from the holding cell however, someone had obviously given him hair gel or some agent which he used to get it standing upright, much like one would describe as a 'crew cut'.

I remonstrated with his solicitor who must have researched the situation beforehand and challenged me to find a directive that he couldn't use his hair style in that way. Of course, how a prisoner presents himself on an ID parade, is pretty much up to him. Needless to say, none of the witnesses were able to identify him.

Anyway, the tribunal had lasted three days between 10th – 12th October 1994, a matter of a few weeks before my retirement. I had obviously spent a huge amount of time in preparation for presenting the case against the officer but, of course, for the reasons stated above, it was very difficult. I called my evidence during the first two days and on the final day, 12th October, the then retired Detective Chief Superintendent David Cole was called to the witness box by the charged officer.

I cross examined him but there was not a great deal to be adduced other than that he had been the Senior Investigating Officer responsible for the investigation. (Which was pretty important) It was then following a heartfelt verbal statement given by the charged officer, that without the need for any further evidence to be heard, the chairman declared that he had already discussed the case with the two Police Complaints Authority members and they were of the unanimous belief that the officer had no case to answer. He was duly released from the tribunal and continued to work with the excellent reputation that he had already gained before this tragic affair started.

Was it not a travesty then, that this officer and his family were put through the months of worry they had obviously endured only to be told by the very authority that had directed his tribunal, that he had no case to answer? The very same statement as advised to them by Mr Blakey, the Chief Constable.

Would this also not represent a huge kick in the teeth for Marie's husband and family. They had been the victims on two counts but of course, when it comes to dishing out fairness, the wheels of justice appear only to turn in the direction of the accused and never towards the victim. The Police Complaints Authority had, of course, protected their backs in at least putting someone in jeopardy of being blamed, and could wash their hands about the end result.

The failure to disclose the tape evidence, (however caused) from the trial had caused Browning's release. However, in the eyes of many, he had escaped justice and justice had escaped the Wilks family. It was to be that in 2018, Browning died suddenly at his home in Wales. It was unfortunately not long after, that the Detective Chief Inspector who faced the disciplinary tribunal, collapsed and died suddenly at his home. There were no winners.

13.

JUDGES RULES and the

THE POLICE AND CRIMINAL EVIDENCE ACT 1984

I have mentioned the above M50 murder case specifically to introduce the huge change which came more to the end of my service but which I consider has helped the criminal no end by causing the hands of those tasked to investigate them, being tied behind their backs.

Typically, the changes came about as a result of officers bending what was then called the 'Judges Rules' to suit their purposes. The changes could therefore be described as 'own goals'. One can hardly fail to remember the awful headlines in the press during the first year of my service in 1963. Some of the grimmest known episodes of violence and corruption within a British police force took place inside Sheffield's Water Street Police Station's interview room. This is where detectives brutally beat suspects with stolen weapons, including a "rhino whip", and fabricated evidence to frame them. An inquiry into the "rhino whip affair" found the leadership of the force was involved. The chief constable retired days later.

Other similar, but perhaps not so high-profile examples followed.

The Judges' Rules were not rules of law, but rather rules of practice for Police guidance, setting out the conduct that would cause a judge to exercise discretion to exclude evidence, in the interests of a fair trial. I have no apology to make in referring to an excellent article written by Col. T. E. St. Johnston, C. B. E., M.A., who had served as Chief Constable of Lancashire for 25 years. Colonel Johnston was an academic who served in the British

Police from 1930. He was also a Barrister-at-Law and had lectured on the subject of Police Administration in the United States.

His article was about the problems of police interrogation, the restrictions, the rules and the administrative directions concerning by and large, the proposition that a confession is admissible at a trial only if it was made voluntarily and without inducements, threats, tricks, or force. It was published in the Criminal Law Journal in 1966, at a time during my own early career as a constable.

The article commences by him saying that the methods used in the interrogation of suspected persons and the value of evidence thus obtained had long been the subject of comment, both judicial and otherwise. There were no rules which governed investigations and it was not until later that some form of guidance was given to the police when questioning persons suspected of, or charged with crime.

At the beginning of the twentieth century, senior police officers became alarmed at the criticisms levied at them. Finally, in 1906 matters came to a head when one Chief Constable wrote to the Lord Chief Justice asking him to give a ruling, clarifying the circumstances in which a caution should be used. One Chief Constable complained that a judge had criticised a constable for using it; and another Judge, in similar circumstances, had criticised a constable for omitting it.

Following this, many similar requests were made until 1912 when the Judges formulated the first four Judges' Rules. In 1918 they prepared another five rules and in 1930, issued a statement clearing points of ambiguity in the nine rules they had made.

It was not until 1947 and 1948, that additional guidance concerning the service of confessions on a co-accused were received from the Home Secretary.

Great emphasis was placed on when, in the course of questioning, any suspect should be cautioned that they need not say anything unless they wished to do so and that whatever they said would be put into writing and given in evidence. The caution should also be given again, immediately following their being charged with any offence.

The accompanying 'Administrative Directions' dealt with the actual recording of statements, pocket book recordings of conversations with suspects being maintained, notes being taken at times of interviewing and any breaks in between, refreshments provided etc. These were all such matters which, those making them, who perhaps had never interviewed a suspect, hoped would fully conclude that suspects would be treated fairly.

When researching this and reminding myself that one of the rules concerned the fact that no alcoholic refreshment shall be given to suspects, I developed a large grin. They had clearly not thought of the possibility of my Stan Ruck being falsely released on bail so that he could get a belly full of cider down him before confessing his crime!

The above is just a small fraction of the content of Colonel Johnston's article but I trust it's sufficient to convey the spirit of it. Unfortunately, the 1960s period I previously referred to was about the same time as gang warfare erupted in London with such names as 'The Richardson gang, the Kray twins with Frankie Fraser and other numerous notorious criminals running riot in London torturing their enemies by cutting off toes and extracting teeth. (Whether they were decayed or not). One can imagine the result of interviewing one of these suspects after they had been told that they "need not say anything unless they wished to do so".

Yes, the 'Rhino Whip' type incidents would be no more and a good job too. Those involved had clearly overstepped the line in their misdirected belief that justice would be served. However, the cost of that would be bound to have an effect on justice as a whole. Surely the eventual introduction of the measures to stop them as contained within the Police and Criminal Evidence Act 1984 (PACE) would become the largest ever hammer required to crack nuts.

To say that no trickery or 'deals' were struck at such interviews even after those notorious cases were reported, would be unbelievable, so the penalty to be paid would surely land on the desks of every Chief Constable and it was to be a hefty one.

Yes, whilst Stan Ruck and others I had dealt with were on the bottom rung of notoriety and criminality, these problem gangs were at the top end of that ladder. However, it was the petty thieves and burglars that all police forces were to continue dealing with every day of the year. Their numbers were 99.99% more than these notorious type gangs I've mentioned above but of course, no matter how petty they were, the same rules were going to have to be applied in every strict detail. They were soon to catch on that every day was their birthday!

No Comment Interviews and 'The Verbals'.

But whilst some of these petty criminals were affable characters, many of them were 'nasty' people responsible for 'nasty' crimes. This, sometimes coupled with the investigator's irrefutable knowledge that the suspect he faced committed the crime but also knowing that without a confession, a conviction would be improbable, was frustrating to say the least. More often than not, the police informer's identity needed to be preserved and "No Comment", "No Comment" and more "No Comment" were the phrases that might keep him or her awake at night.

So, could it be believed that after the uproar of the 'Rhino Whip' affair etc. that inducements or deals would not continue to be used? Also, could it still be believed that the notes of interviews made during the interviews were notes meticulously taken down during the interviews or shortly after them? Without a tape recorder being present, I challenge anyone to hold a fast and flowing conversation with anyone, least a suspect, for even five minutes, let alone the hours that interviews can last for, and then to record the details of that interview either contemporaneously or soon afterwards.

I would contend that it is not possible to record verbatim contemporaneous notes but of course, it was the words, *'shortly afterwards'* which became the 'get out of jail' card but which obviously opened the gate for 'the verbals' to be alleged by suspects whether they were used or not.

For those not too familiar with the term, 'verbals', to record that a suspect had said, **"OK Guv, it's a fair cop"** when he had vehemently denied any knowledge of the crime is just a good, though over exaggerated example of using the 'verbals' – In plain terms, telling lies about what a suspect had said.

I doubt that such an example was ever used but the gate was still open for both the investigators to use more subtle phrases and also for the suspect to falsely contend that what was recorded, was not what he or she said at all, even though it was.

To record what was said during an interview with a suspect who genuinely directly admitted guilt or inferred his or her guilt, isn't as easy as it might appear. I could describe many examples of this and recall on one occasion as a Detective Chief Inspector, getting together for hours with my Detective Inspector following a series of very long interviews conducted during a murder at Kidderminster.

The note taking, indeed assuming notes were taken at the time, will inevitably be sparse and sometimes almost non-existent and more so perhaps 'illegible' when rapid responses are required, but it would have given us a short-hand sequence of the pertinent links in the conversations which would enable us to write up our notes. To complicate matters in the example I have in mind, two suspects were being held and through necessity, it meant that the second suspect was required to be interviewed at a time during the first suspect's interview. In short, we needed to suspend the first interview to interview the other suspect before returning to the first.

This was a pattern which occurred on more than one occasion and without the Detective Inspector's shorthand notes, we would have been lost. Whilst no admissions were forthcoming, the suspects replied to every question put to them because they had hatched an alibi which required them to present it when questioned.

The alibi was very much over-egged with a complicated description of their whereabouts and timings through many different scenarios which although real, were mistimed and which eventually led to their convictions at Oxford Crown Court. However, I can say here and now that if they had decided on 'NO COMMENT' interviews, we would have struggled and they may have well escaped justice.

So, it must be obvious that not all of the conversations held, would be recorded. There would be the peripheral build up to the meat of the interview, numerous statements about things not pertinent to the enquiry but in the end, those things that were pertinent to the crux of the interview have obviously to be broached. These are the problem areas which I have no doubt are those which are open to abuse by both the investigator and suspect as described above. I would be surprised on both counts, if they weren't abused. The only way forward was obviously to be the tape recording and the filming of these interviews.

It is here that I reflect back many chapters to that which I've previously mentioned about the television programme portrayals of real police interviews. If I had been blessed with a full head of hair, then when these first aired and started to be commonplace, I would have torn it all out.

First of all, I can't believe that the police hierarchy had thought it wise to allow these tapes to be used for the production of such programmes. I would love to know how on earth that happened. Secondly, what the public, including the criminals among them, were seeing, was to teach them that all they had to do was sit back, often yawning at the investigator's questions and say 'NO COMMENT' to each question. I ask myself, "Is this Justice"?

Hasn't anyone understood that if one is innocent of the reason behind their arrest, then why should they have no comments to make? They ought to be shouting their innocence from the highest roof.

Never in a month of Sundays can it be justice: I would even go as far as to question why, when a person is suspected of a crime, must he be told that he need not say anything? The police are allowed to ask anyone questions, suspects and innocent people alike. So why should it be that suspects are afforded the pleasure, and yes, the huge advantage of not having to answer the questions put to them? Why then are the police allowed to question anybody in the course of their investigations when those they question are allowed not to answer the questions put to them? It just doesn't make sense.

Surely, not answering must infer some guilt? By the same token, if they have nothing to hide, then what is it that makes them not want to help the police in solving the crime? Not to answer questions is surely a manipulation of the process of justice.

So, not only have we advertised the fact that our lawmakers have been naïve, we have shouted to the world that freedom has, in many instances, been granted to law breakers because of their naivety. The system now has the appearance of deliberate obstruction to the police's pursuit of evidence to catch those who do not care for the hurt they cause their victims. Those responsible for such one-sided legal protection for criminals, should be made to sit down again and watch the documentaries such as 'Real CSI' which concern real criminal investigations. Perhaps they may now realise how they have provided a charter for criminality. It is these cases which demonstrate that without forensic evidence, there is little chance of detecting these crimes, let alone persuading suspects to admit their responsibilities.

They may also realise that all the criminals watching such programmes, will be rubbing their hands in glee to learn of such methods. The tips they will have learned is tantamount to them attending a course entitled, 'How to evade being caught'.

I've viewed many of the cases portrayed on this program and so far as documentaries are concerned, I think their portrayal of the cases are brilliant. However, in addition to most all premeditated crimes being committed by the wearing of gloves, they will now be burning all their clothes, cleaning up any 'contact' traces and showering after committing their crimes. These methods will not only be adopted by the 'upper echelon' of criminality but the regular petty criminals, perhaps with long previous convictions, who will be doing the same in their efforts to evade justice.

Also, whilst it has been useful to portray the silence of these suspects to highlight the problem, was there otherwise a reason for showing them? Maybe the producers are doing so to support and guide their viewers' beliefs in the guilt of those being interviewed. But surely, the fact that just about every suspect adopts this tactic, demonstrates how they have become advertisements to others to do the same? Not showing such interviews would not have been detrimental to the quality of the programmes and surely all that needs to be said is that the suspect refused to answer questions or admit their guilt. Is it any wonder that crime detection rates are tumbling and the police are now criticised for their inaction?

To repeat, I cannot believe why the recordings of these interviews have ever been released by the police forces concerned. I'm absolutely sure that the Chief Constables I have worked with, would have resisted all efforts by these film companies to take possession of them.

In my opinion, these changes which, after all, have occurred to ostensibly increase the public's education and entertainment, have caused the shape of policing to have become warped out of all proportion. I'm almost sure it's not the case, but this does make me wonder whether money crossing palms has been a persuasive element in such matters for police forces who are almost always strapped for funds.

WE HAVE MOST CERTAINLY 'LOST IT' and unlike the previous Judges Rules with its lack of belt and braces approach preventing the abuses witnessed, the Police and Criminal Evidence Act 1984, has more than caused every chink and hollow in them, to be plugged to such an extent that suspects now being interviewed have been allowed the upper hand.

Not only would the 'PRE-PACE' interviewer be seeking a confession for the crime arrested, but there was competition among both uniform and detective officers concerning the number of similar cases which could be detected through such interview processes.

Offenders could opt to have other offences written off to them as being 'Taken into Consideration' when sentenced. After sentencing, they could also be visited in prison on a later date to sign a confession which would cause various crimes to be legally 'written off' as detected to those prisoners.

The principle in being, was that owing to the suspect already serving a sentence, it would not be in the public interest to arrest and charge the prisoner with additional offences committed before his sentence. These procedures might well act as a huge lever in persuading suspects to admit the offences they had committed in the past. They would, in effect, be 'wiping their slate clean'. This was not trickery, but the use of legal processes which, when presented properly, may well be regarded as a 'good deal' to those sitting on the opposite side of the table.

But of course, many of those who supported these changes will point out that those suspected of committing a crime have been cautioned that they need not say anything. But as will be discussed later, some of those judges who agreed upon the caution being given, held the view that so long as the suspect and those interviewing them were on **'even terms'**, there was no need to administer the caution in the first place.

The definition of 'even terms' does of course, become critical and the fact that an interview is being recorded and videoed is surely to be more than sufficient to equate to its being held on 'even terms'. How could it not?

However, it is almost unbelievable that five years following the introduction of PACE, in 1989, the West Midlands Police disbanded its Serious Crime Squad following the discovery that in a series of around 100 criminal cases, its members had been shown to have been tampering with statement evidence to secure convictions. I'm not sure what level of admissions or otherwise would have occurred during the interviews, but it certainly appears once again that the police had shot themselves in the foot.

The sad part about these changing shapes of policing, is the effect it has had on the genuinely honest police officers, (which I know they mostly are) in that the motivation to detect crime in general has waned. No longer is it a game of cat and mouse, no longer are the police pitting their wits against the run of the mill petty thieves and burglars. Yes, in contravention of 'Judges Rules', there was always a means of persuasion to 'cough' that could be used.

The hint of favours and promises were bound to be made. It was also productive to use the type of language and vernacular used by the suspect. This might also involve the same level of blue language used by the suspect. He or she needed to be spoken to in a language which they understood and was 'normal' to them. So far as I was concerned, the 'Good Cop / Bad Cop' was a tactic mainly for film directors, but occasionally, it might appear in a genuine scenario.

So now that these interviews are filmed and recorded, there is no way that varying styles of interviewing can be adopted by the interviewer. They can only be 'straight up and down' questioning for the hope of an answer which might help detect the offence. Officers must be very careful not to offer inducements of any kind and even discounting the crude interference with statements as referred to above, the recording and eventual videoing of police interviews will have stopped any infringements of the evidence gathering and interview rules prescribed by PACE. Whilst some notes continued to be taken, the full interview is recorded for all to hear and see, so the verbal accusations by both sides have immediately been blocked. The so-called 'dodgy' skills of interviewing were stymied.

The 'Pre-Pace' competition was not only fought between prisoner and interviewer but collectively between one night shift against another, or even one Police Division against others. These were the only benefits achieved and reflected not only on one's ability or skill as an interviewer but as a measure of the efficiency performed by themselves and their particular shift of officers.

At the start of a week on a night shift, it was a normal occurrence to go through the charge book to quickly count the number of arrests the previous shift had made during their week's shift of nights. Such gains were not sufficient to create any form of corruption or personal gain. But alas, 'The baby had been thrown out with the bathwater' and I can understand why our communities at large are left to suffer escalating levels of serious crimes, because of the scoring of these 'own goals'.

The appointment of Custody Sergeants has prevented the interviewing of prisoners 'off the record' as far as possible. Promises to the future or deals are things of the past. Constraints on the time suspects are allowed to be kept in custody without charge, are only to be extended by a Superintendent and later, a court hearing. This undoubtedly would hinder the investigation. No longer will suspects be held on a wing and a prayer and if arrested, no longer would they be legally held in police cells over weekends or even overnight until the investigators returned on duty, as was previously the case.

No way do I intend to infer that false trickery be used to place suspects in peril of being falsely accused but it must be said that all these measures have been introduced because of the actions of the few and therefore, one cannot argue that they are not just. However, it hurts to have to say that, especially when these culprits have used far worse trickery, fraud and sometimes brutality on those that have suffered the consequences of their actions. We have got ourselves into a position where we are protecting the 'baddies' and leaving the 'goodies' to the wolves!

Balancing the Scales of Justice

The only areas where the balance of justice has slightly moved in the police's favour have been the mostly scientific advances made in such things as DNA analysis, CCTV camera installations, computer and mobile telephone forensics, data tracking, listening devices, vehicle tracking devices, computerised intelligence gathering and dissemination, automatic number plate recognition and fingerprint identification systems. The need for forensic science to be applied to cases has never been more desirable because without such evidence, criminals are walking away from justice and laughing about it.

Some of these things had already been in place but some required special permission to deploy. They are very helpful but it saddens me to hear from current police officers that the skills of interviewing have long ago passed by and all that is required of them today is to put the evidence to the suspect including basically asking them if they had committed the crime. Whilst they may choose to answer some questions, as soon as the going gets tough , TV has taught them that all they have to say is 'NO COMMENT'.

Whilst accepting that the tiniest proportion of our practitioners' have been proved to be corrupt, or at least their actions being synonymous to bad policing, those ensuing changes have been made generally, for the betterment of the Justice system. However, the fact that they have caused so much change resulting in the pendulum of justice swinging so far away from the police who are there to protect us, makes my verdict upon them to be a resounding disapproval. However, one has to accept that our beds have been made by the few, and that we must all lie in them, but surely, those beds can be made more comfortable in the furtherance of justice.

Sadly, it is difficult to see any solution to that problem on the near horizon. However, in my conclusions below, I have suggested a course of action which, if adopted, may cause that pendulum of justice to swing somewhere closer to where it should be.

14.

THE CROWN PROSECUTION SERVICE

I have already made many references in early chapters to Magistrates Courts which, in past times, had been commonly known as 'The Police Courts'. These were scattered all over the country in which local people were tried and judged by local magistrates who possessed local knowledge, especially of the area of their jurisdiction, and often (rightly or wrongly) of those who faced them.

As far as the prosecutions being heard in them were concerned, the Magistrates Clerks department worked with police divisional personnel, in a large department in each Division, called, would you believe, 'The Prosecutions Department'. This would be responsible for the processing of prosecution files which ended up in these courts. Other of their duties were to attend to the court listings in conjunction with magistrates clerks departments so that witnesses could be warned and called to attend court as and when required.

I have also mentioned that Inspectors would also normally be assigned to prosecute the more straightforward business in these courts but occasionally, for more protracted, often 'Not Guilty' plea cases, a local solicitor would be hired to perform those prosecutions.

My experience of prosecuting cases commenced in the Sergeant rank when the allotted Inspector in either the Worcester County Court or the Droitwich town court was unavailable. This was obviously a very public affair and what with the magistrates and their clerks, the press, defence lawyers and often members of the public in the gallery, it represented quite a responsible duty, far removed from my normal duties and in all honesty, when I first started prosecuting, it frightened the living daylights out of me.

The occasions on which I did this duty were not infrequent and, of course, when I became the Inspector, deputy to the County Sub Divisional Commander, I regularly prosecuted two courts per week.

In addition to the actual court work, much effort needed to be expended not only by the officers who had earlier performed the arrests or the reporting of offenders for a summons. It was also a time-absorbing duty and tiresome business performed by supervisors who were working in the chain of consideration about what should happen to the alleged offenders. With juvenile offenders, consultation was later required with the probation departments (later Juvenile panels) as to the best way to deal with these juvenile delinquents.

Most decisions were straightforward enough but the juveniles were much more complicated. Most files involving juveniles comprised many alleged offenders. Some may have been involved in all of the offences listed whilst others may not. Those that were not, might be involved with a particular group of others, some of which were involved with other juveniles in different offences. (Work that one out!) I remember that it was often necessary to draw up a matrix on a scrap of paper so as to be able to capture who was involved with whom and with what offence or offences. It was a nightmare.

It was on 15th May 1984 when, as a Superintendent at Bromsgrove, I had been wrestling with one of these giant files for some time and many of the offences featured various children of a family called Badley. (Not their true name). They lived not far from the Police Station. No matter where one police's, there will always be one or two notorious families that come to notice more frequently than others. At Bromsgrove, these were the Badleys.

I was so fed up and frustrated with this family that I recall slapping my pen down on the file I was studying and with the duty Inspector, we walked to their home where I intended to hand out some instant cautions with some choice language. (Oh, OK – Bollockings) The file I had been looking through provided me with sufficient ammunition to lay the law down.

Low and behold, as we walked we heard messages over our radios to the effect that some of the 'Badley Kids' were trespassing on an Industrial Unit, the property of a particular 'Light Engineering Company'. This helped to boil my blood at even a higher temperature and we soon reached the front door of this huge family. Thankfully Mr. Badley (senior) opened it and I let him have both barrels. My heated conversation was, I suppose, tantamount to a threat to have his kids 'taken into 'Care' or at least locked up if he could not adequately discipline and supervise them.

I went through the information I had gleaned from the file and I told him that I would not make a decision until a fixed time had elapsed. I was to hold a 'sword of Damocles' over his head like a suspended sentence.

Having aired my concern, we started to walk back to the Station when over the radio came information that an unregistered motor bike with no silencer was being ridden on private land and on public pavements near to the Dolphin Swimming Baths. We calculated that the direction of reported travel would bring the machine close to where we were and so we stood in the shadows and waited. It wasn't long before we could hear the thing.

It was young Martin Badley, one of the kids who had featured in the file I had been studying. We were just across the road from his home and because he had no documents for the machine whatsoever, I told him to carry it across the road without letting any part of it touch the road or else he would be prosecuted for having no Insurance for it as well as the many other driving offences involved.

I had had enough. I had been out on patrol for probably less than an hour and my hopes that the Badleys would not be heard of again were shattered. Although young Martin hadn't had time to be told of my visit by his father, I probably believed that it wouldn't make any difference and so, when I returned, I again picked up my pen and wrote up the file to the effect that at least all Badleys concerned should be prosecuted. I would add that there was no satisfaction in doing this because their upbringing was entirely the work of their parents and possibly their grandparents before them. The kids were to suffer but there were few other options to consider. Cautions had been tried and failed many, many times before. There may lie another brick dislodged from that wall. Could cautioning juveniles for 15 – 20 times for their criminal activity really be the way to stop them re-offending?

There of course, came a time when the view, in my opinion, quite rightly dictated that as it was the police who normally first instigated the appearance of those in court, that the process could do with a taste of Independence. You got booked or arrested by the police, you got bailed or summoned to attend court through police decisions and then when in court, you were also prosecuted by them.

In addition, the sheer number of prosecutions, not helped by adjournments for one reason or another, saw the courts becoming overcrowded and swamped with business. Police were being criticised for bringing cases to court on 'a wing and a prayer' was the parlance used. Trials could take up court time for a whole day or more and other cases would inevitably be 'put back' in the lists. In short, the system became nothing better than 'a mess'!

As a major cog in the wheel of decisions to prosecute, I can confess that considerations of court time did not have any influence on the decisions I made. With good hunches that offenders were guilty, albeit on flimsy or circumstantial evidence, I would often write – 'Let the court decide' and mark the file up for prosecution. My view was that it was justice which ought to have taken precedence over court time.

So, inevitably, The Crown Prosecution Service was inaugurated and it was in 1986, at the time when I was employed with Her Majesty's Inspectorate of Constabulary that this huge change occurred. I mention this because the actual setting up of it was something of a disaster. Unlike our Prosecutions Departments, they weren't allowed to have their premises in any police accommodation. The funds forming their budgets were inadequate and I think I'm correct in saying that two of the Chief Crown Prosecutors appointed for their regions, had committed suicide due to their worries about creating their particular departments.

The other early problems concerned the lack of professionalism often displayed by their solicitor employees. On reflection, why would a solicitor want to be employed in such an organisation, when they could work up to maybe a partnership in an established firm? In that context, many were young and junior in experience and quickly left to join such firms. It was difficult, because many firms had amalgamated after losing such work when the 'legal aid green card' was severely curtailed. In short, the 'turnover' of staff was constant it didn't help when they often earned the wrath of magistrates who also didn't enjoy the change.

Early problems were inevitably ironed out and now, this agency, headed by the Director of Public Prosecutions, employs 5,794 people (2019 / 20 stats.) and in 2013, had an annual budget of over £590 million. It decides which cases should be prosecuted, determines the appropriate charges in more serious or complex cases, and advises the police during the early stages of investigations and prepares cases presenting them at court.

One of their early challenges was to reduce the backlog of cases to be prosecuted. This was partially attempted by withdrawing many cases and then only prosecuting cases which had a reasonable chance of succeeding. The CPS statement says: -

- Does the evidence provide a realistic prospect of conviction? That means, having heard the evidence, is a court more likely than not to find the defendant guilty? And;
- Is it in the public interest to prosecute? That means asking questions including how serious the offence is, the harm caused to the victim, the impact on communities and whether prosecution is a proportionate response.

No longer would those 'let the court decide' cases be pursued under this decision-making process. It was fortunate for me that many years later in

2003, I found myself in a position to witness myself what this meant in practical terms.

Prior to the introduction of the CPS, many forces had taken on a new concept of compiling prosecution files through 'Administrative Support Units'. (ASUs) The basic idea was that following initial arrests being made, the officer/s involved would hand over a short report and any accompanying papers, to these ASUs which were staffed by officers who had proven track records in evidence gathering and the compilation of process files. The benefit of this was that the files would be more accurately completed and the arresting officers would be quickly released to be able to return to their primary job on their various beats. This aspect of our work will be discussed at more depth in the next chapter.

However, their function, by 2003 had been slightly amended to include the submission of files to the CPS. Any additional work required, or contact with the officers involved, would be made through this office which by then, I had learned, had been changed to the CJSU Offices, (Criminal Justice Support Unit).

So it was, that when I had enrolled into the 'Retained Experienced Personnel' scheme, in May 2003, I was asked to work in the Redditch CJSU which, by a huge coincidence, was housed in what had been my own office when I worked there as a Chief Superintendent in command of the 'B' Division of West Mercia. I had already been employed in analysing crime reports as earlier discussed, so that experience was now being extended to actually examining the files which were being submitted to the CPS and answering any queries which they might return.

In short, I was often absolutely flabbergasted, not only by the poor work intended for submission to the CPS but by the actions of the CPS which by their own submissions, showed how inept they were. There were many examples I could give but uppermost in my mind after all these 18 years have passed by, concerned a young couple falling out over money issues.

Because he was so upset, the husband drew many £50 notes out of the bank, got drunk and drove his wife's car into the shop front of the hairdressers in which she worked. He decamped and was later found at their home, still in a drunken state. He had ripped up some £50 notes leaving some pieces of them in the car, other pieces of them were found in his possession, together with his wife's car keys. He had been charged with the taking of his wife's car without consent, and all the 'drink drive' offences involved. His wife wanted rid of him and fully supported the prosecution.

To cut a detailed story very short, not to include all the whys and wherefores which are now hazy in my mind, the CPS had decided that as there was no evidence from anyone who actually saw him driving the car, they would not prosecute him. This landed on my desk and I saw red. I could not believe the decision made and was so angry that, even though I was now only a temporary junior clerk, I took the decision to write to the Chief Prosecuting Officer at Droitwich with a copy of the file containing the decision. To again cut this story short, the defendant ended up in court and was 'potted'.

So in conclusion, the question must be asked, "Was this change to an independent prosecution system, a worthwhile one? For sure, the objective of reducing the backlog of cases to court was achieved, but at what cost? I feel that the idea of independence in the process was a fair one, but made for the wrong reasons. It surely wasn't the job of a police officer to stand in court with professionals in other disciplines to prosecute cases. For a start, none of us doing that had received any training for the job and basically learned as we went along.

The negative aspects of the change were many. Firstly, magistrates courts lost their 'local' feel about them and resulting from mergers, defendants, witnesses and even the magistrates sometimes now have long journeys, often many miles away from their homes, to attend courts. I was recently informed by a retired JP friend of mine that he was asked to travel to Cheshire in order to make up a bench which had been hit by absences. This would have involved a round trip of about 100 miles.

The most serious charge I have to lay at the change, however, is the fact that it has caused more crimes to be committed and more criminals not to be prosecuted.

I'm sure this state of affairs wasn't envisaged when the plan to introduce the CPS was first conceived, but in their efforts to reduce court time etc, there are now many more cases which never get near a court. Over the years, criminals now know that their destiny can also rely on the CPS not prosecuting them. They have come to realise that unless they confess to the police, the chances are that they will get away with their criminal activity. So now, with that brick wall in mind. What with PACE having already built a wall between the criminal and the likelihood of them being charged, an additional wall has been built between the CPS and the likelihood of a court appearance.

In addition, even if in the first instance, the CPS approve proceedings, should it later be made clear that the defendant will contest the issue, the CPS may revert their decision and withdraw the charges or downgrade them, so as not to be involved in a lengthy 'not guilty' trial.

Surely this means that criminals are likely to feel more confident that they won't be punished for their crimes which therefore must lead to them committing more of them?

Another negative aspect surfaces when one discusses such issues with officers who have worked under this system and who may continue for some time to do so. It has served to add to the death of the 'competitive spirit' involved in the detection of crime which had hitherto existed as earlier described. Sadly, all this has now culminated in Police Officers believing that these duties have now become 'just a job' and not a 'vocation'. *"We'll ask them if they've done it and when they deny that they have, what else can we do"* is the type of response I have received.

What with PACE and the CPS knocking back their cases by withdrawing charges, even if they had once approved them or even discontinuing other minor charges, the will to get involved in such work with such a spirit, is now virtually dead.

Waiting lists in UK courts and hospitals reach record levels

The Financial Times – November 2020

The above headline was produced as a Covid 19 Impact story and so would cloud the issue in normal times. I am not privileged to know whether magistrates or crown courts had previously enjoyed shorter waiting lists but I know where my money would be placed if I was asked to gamble. The objective of getting cases to court on time has now most probably worsened instead of improved.

15.

ADMINISTRATION SUPPORT UNITS

As previously mentioned, the ASUs appeared shortly before I was appointed to join the staff at Her Majesty's Inspectorate of Constabulary. We had been informed at a management meeting that one of my Chief Superintendent colleagues, Peter Murphy, had been to the Metropolitan Police to have a look at this concept. He was then the head of the 'Systems Development Department' so the scrutiny of this idea of improving and speeding up the production of files for onward transmission to the prosecution stage, naturally fell into his lap.

We were later to receive a far deeper understanding of it, and agreed that on the face of it, experience was sorely lacking in both areas of evidence gathering and file preparation, and it was generally welcomed that to cream off the best officers in these fields, to take this over was a good idea.

Having now been appointed as staff officer to Mr. John (later Sir John) Woodcock, I understood that the 'Police Efficiency Unit' at the Home Office, also wished to take on board this concept and asked all five of the Regional HMIs, to encourage their use during force inspections.

I'd better explain first, that all forces inspected would first receive a visit from a staff officer to conduct a 'Pre-Inspection' about a month or so prior to the HMI's Inspection proper. These would last two or three weeks, far longer than the inspections themselves. We would be armed with all the directives which the Home Office would want to be addressed in the post inspection performance report. This was, of course, a prerequisite to forces receiving the Home Office grant. The Staff Officer's 'Pre-Inspection' report would be submitted to their respective HMIs and to be honest, whilst this was designed to be a brief for him, we hoped that it would resemble the final report he would sign off. The benefit of the Pre-Inspection was that officer's in force would be more likely to divulge not only their 'best practice' but their concerns also.

> *To interject here, my briefs to the HMI did not fall into the category of being 'brief' at all. (As readers of this book might expect) Sir John often accused me of trying to write the full report which should result from the actual inspection. I plead guilty to this in part, but not in total, however, with a smile on his face, he often reminded me about it. With my two-year secondment to him coming to an end, I knew that he would throw a 'farewell' party for me at his home and in his speech, I could guarantee, that the briefness (or not) of my briefs to him would be mentioned and that above all, he would accuse me of not knowing the meaning of the word 'brief'.*

> *So, I went to Marks and Spencer and bought a packet of two gents briefs and stuck them in my back pocket at my farewell do. As anticipated, out poured my lack of knowledge about the meaning of the word 'Brief' and my plan to scope what would be near to his final report to the Home Office.*

> *Then, of course, it was my turn and I was able to utter my response about that aspect. I exclaimed that I was utterly disappointed in the highest paid and most experienced and respected ex Chief Constable not knowing what the definition of 'brief' was. "Shouldn't he be ashamed"? I asked. I withdrew the packet of briefs from my pocket and said, "Well, in my desperation to show him what a brief looked like, I have bought him not one, but two pairs of briefs so that he shall never forget"!*

So back to the subject of ASUs, during my pre-inspections, I had picked up early concerns in a couple of forces that creaming off the competent officers who were good evidence gatherers and report compilers, was having the effect of leaving the majority of officers not in the ASUs, without gaining any experience at all in those areas. They would ask, "Who's going to replace the ASU officers when they leave their ASU for whatever reason"?

I had already had a taste of a similar problem on my first promotion to sergeant when I was posted at Worcester, which had not long been amalgamated from being a 'City' force on its own and where, as a consequence, sufficient personnel were employed in a small area, to form specialist squads for just about every role other than walking the beat and looking smart. It became a joke that during the rush hour every road junction between the station and the Chief Super's home would be manned so that traffic wouldn't hold him up on his way home. And if traffic were light, he would receive a smart salute as he passed.

Within the confines of the city, they had their own traffic division for attending road accidents, CID for dealing with all crimes reported, Coroner's Officer for dealing with all deaths etc. and so on my arrival, I quickly realised that my sergeant colleagues in what had been a 'City' force, were having difficulty in carrying out the duties, which us constables in Herefordshire, a 'County' force, had been performing for years. I quickly became their best friend and the source of lots of information, such as, for example, how to deal with applications to make building alterations to licensed premises which required the 'Licensing Justices' consent.

These sergeants had been used to having a 'Licensing Department' whose officers would deal with all aspects of licensed premises. Worcester City had now been amalgamated not only into a 'county' type division, but into one much larger force that involved three counties. As a consequence, it wasn't long before the surfeit of 'specialist' officers was shared out among those stations who had not been so lucky as them. They were going to have to operate in the same fashion as their county cousins and I was lucky enough to be one of them.

This was obviously not their fault because their system grew as a result of always being up to staff establishment. Even after amalgamation, those who had joined the Worcester City force were entitled by regulation to remain serving and living within the city boundary until they agreed to surrender

202

that right, mostly in the end, on promotion. This state of affairs also had similarly evolved in the Metropolitan Force, so the idea of specialists for taking statements and compiling prosecution files, was for them, also a good one. They had been allowed to travel many miles from home to station whereas us 'county coppers' were required to live on the patch we worked, as directed by the Chief.

From the very start, for the above reason of selectivity , I wasn't so keen on the idea and I began whispering concerns about it in the HMI's ear. There were very few occasions indeed, when our views weren't in unison with each other. Perhaps this and the extent of 'Civilianisation' within the forces, was the only other one. He would have none of it. I suppose for him, it would have been like pushing against the Home Office tide and of course, what he believed in.

So eighteen years later when as described in the last chapter, I was asked as a 'Retired Experienced Personnel' to work in what they now called, the Criminal Justice Support Unit (CJSU), I found the system was just the same as previously described but now, of course, the Crown Prosecutions Department was pulling the strings with regard to all aspects of charges, and court file preparation.

The lines of communication relative to the compilation and the submission of files had become blocked and completely out of sync with court appearances etc. In short, it was another mess.

I hate to say *"I told you so"*, but a huge problem existed with arresting officers not being experienced enough to obtain decent witness statements or to further compile their prosecution files. Officers attached to these CJSUs were flooded with work and sinking under the strain. Also, as described in the previous chapter, the CPS were being measured on the number of discontinuances they mandated and the number of charges which they would not support. I could go on, but I guess I was just fortunate enough to be alive after those eighteen years had elapsed and that, from the very office I had sat in as the Divisional Commander, all those years ago,

I could now see the sad end result of this so-called experiment, or specialisation, which hadn't curried favour with me as described above.

Was it no wonder that during those occasions when, also under the 'REP' scheme, I was asked to analyse the crimes being submitted by uniformed officers through interrogating their computerised 'CRIMES' system, that I discovered that on many occasions, it had been the blind leading the blind? I think not. For if prosecution files weren't being compiled and submitted by them, how would they get to learn exactly what is required? I'll rest my case there.

16.

POLICE CIVILIANISATION

For as many years as I can remember, there had been numerous tasks performed by officers who really did not need a warrant card to complete them. One of the hidden benefits of this was that officers who had become medically unfit to carry out police duties, were often sucked into police stations to carry them out. This, of course, was viewed as a considerable benefit to those who may otherwise have been retired from the force on medical grounds and depending upon the number of years served, their pension may well not have reached the desired level of those who were able to complete their full pensionable service.

Civilianisation of hitherto, police posts, is therefore viewed with a variety of spectacles depending on one's interest in the financial, political or practical aspects of the process. The Home Office and Local Authorities would obviously be rubbing their hands together at the funds that could be saved; to a certain extent, the police service would be pleased at the release of police officers to help them perform their duties and so far as the public are concerned, there would be benefits of this and of the saving in the taxes they pay. The latter, of course, dependant on them paying taxes and whether or not those savings would be ploughed back into the policing role.

So, the civilianisation of these jobs never really started anywhere near in earnest until the late 1950s but it then gathered momentum after the amalgamation of the smaller forces commencing in the late 1960s.

Traffic Wardens

I can recall that much of my time as a young constable in Hereford was to be employed in keeping the traffic moving by preventing obstructions and thus 'booking' motorists who had either parked where they were not permitted to, or who had overstayed the time limit imposed. In addition, we had a whole battery of yellow 'Police No Waiting' cones which required to be placed out each morning at places lawfully used for parking, but which caused obstructions but weren't covered by 'No Waiting' restrictions. They were also used at many special events where, under normal circumstances, people were able to park.

And so, when Traffic Wardens came on the scene in the 1960s, they were welcomed by the Police with open arms. These were people who had no age or height restrictions to comply with. I can't say that they were similarly welcomed by the motoring members of the public who often suffered from their overzealousness, probably because they had more time to spend on this, their sole task.

Indeed, before receiving my three stripes as a sergeant, I performed the role of a temporary sergeant and wore an arm band containing not three, but two stripes. It was in this role that I became the supervisor of the first batch of Hereford Traffic Wardens when the Sergeant, otherwise in charge of them, took a period of long-term sickness. I recall they were a mixed bunch, some lazy, some scruffy, some ex-military types and others as keen as mustard but on the whole, they were a pleasant bunch who, on most occasions, never deserved the criticisms fired their way.

Civil Enforcement Officers

Now 'Civil Enforcement Officers' are used by Local Authorities to pursue these and local authority owned car parking duties who, almost everywhere, have replaced the "traffic wardens" who were originally part of the local police force.

In 1978, the 'Edmond Davies' pay increase caused police pay to rise by over 100% in the five years between 1977 and 1982. This was 20% over and

206

above the average pay rises in those days. The Police Federation saw the implications probably sooner than anyone else. They assumed rightly, that this might cause the floodgates to open in respect of the possibility of additional civilian employees performing tasks being hitherto, carried out by their police colleagues ……. but at a much cheaper rate.

The Police Advisory Board was made very aware of the Federation's reservations but took no action. Recruitment peaked between 1979 and 1983 but in 1985, this trend began to reverse.

It was in January 1985 when I joined Her Majesty's Police Inspectorate and for the whole two years, one of the many constant directives from the Home Office was the drive towards the civilianisation of police posts. The problem was, that there was no parity between the various forces we inspected. Some were happy to remain as they were, whilst others were civilianising as quickly as they could. Some forces also identified tasks which they considered not worthy of civilianisation, whilst others thought that they were. Whatever, the civilianisation drum was soundly beating and the last I can recall was that most police forces had increased their civilian strength by as much as 50% of their police establishment.

Police and Community Support Officers (PCSOs)

It wasn't until some years after my retirement that the Police Reform Act of 2002 came into force which introduced and formalised the employment of non-warrant card support officers to the police.

The idea that there would be a band of officers dressed clearly in a uniform designed not to be mistaken as police officers, but regarded as the missing link between communities and missing local police beat officers who had sadly by now disappeared, was, in my view, a good one.

The huge problem that I foresaw and which was used by the Police Federation to vehemently fight against the scheme, was that these people would in effect, become police officers employed on the cheap and would thus be replacing their 'Police Federation' members. I recall the debate because although I had handed my warrant card in, I was still employed temporarily in various tasks under the umbrella of the 'Retained Experienced Personnel' scheme. This 'REP' scheme was indeed a very small example of lower paid civilians (Retired Officers) performing duties which could be done by people not in possession of a warrant card.

I recall at first that PCSOs were given very limited police powers and they were not permitted to drive police vehicles. They were simply to be employed as eyes and ears within the community with a rapid communication facility to the regular police should a police presence be required. They were there to replace the void left by those police officers who had by now, been taken off their local beats.

Surely but slowly, they were granted additional powers including the driving of police vehicles. One only has to watch their use in the community and on various television programmes and news casts, to understand that indeed, they are performing many tasks which had hitherto been performed by police officers. As part of my research, my chat with Denise Bushell, an experienced PCSO at Droitwich, confirmed that to be the case but in essence, we were both in agreement that these duties are very often mundane and release the officers to get on with other things.

There were, of course, many other roles which have been taken over by civilian staff in addition to the three large bodies of men and women I have described above. Here are some which immediately spring to mind but there will inevitably be many more which have escaped my memory.

Custody Officers	Police Matrons	Warrant Officers
Administration Depts	Finance Depts	Front Desk Clerks
Telephonists	Dog Kennel staff	Police Trainers
Motor Mechanics	Driving examiners	Vehicle Examiners
Accident Investigators	Scene Examiners	Fingerprint Experts
Control Room Ops	Personnel Officers	Laboratory submission

Not forgetting of course, Coroner's Officers and 'Lost and Found' property clerks.

The question, "Can this role be performed equally as well by anyone without the need for them to have the powers of a constable" is, I believe a good one BUT it is an 'all embracing' question which encompasses some roles which, in hindsight, I would have much preferred to have remained to have been performed by a uniformed police officer. One in particular, which immediately springs to mind, involves those persons who work behind the enquiry desks at police stations.

I have mentioned previously that this was a role often performed by 'Station Sergeants'. These officers not only ruled most of the operational functions of the police station and the officers who were inside them, but also, the public that they greeted. They were normally those who carried themselves well and who possessed a commanding presence. Above all, they had served their time in their various police roles so, were well abreast of the law and the many problems brought to the counters of these larger police stations. They gave the public the confidence that they knew what they were doing.

From that situation, we began to employ members of the public who were never intended to look like police officers and who by their age, appearance and knowledge base, were devoid of such experiences. They were, of course, quite capable of doing many tasks but whilst many of them may have possessed a good local knowledge and could command a good presence, it was highly unlikely that they would have the same knowledge about the law, and more so, the application of it. Station Sergeants would have more than likely dealt with most of the problems brought to their desks and nothing can replace that experience.

This was a view that was indeed shared by the HMI who often said, *"If something is worth reporting to the police at a police station, then those people will be expecting to speak to a police officer when they arrive".* In addition, having reported what they wanted to report , it was very often the case that the 'customer' needed to be referred to a police officer in any event.

The same could be said for those working in control rooms, operations rooms or the plethora of other roles with a variety of names which all involve the interaction with members wishing to report information and the subsequent despatching of police officers to those calls.

The Bromsgrove Sub Division which I commanded as a Superintendent, was one of two sub divisions comprising our Redditch 'B' Division. Within my sub division, I had three police stations all of which had their own telephone numbers, an enquiry desk and a means of directing patrols to incidents.

There came a time when it was decided to operate just one control room which would also be the receiving station for any telephone calls previously made to all three police stations. The financial savings of these mergers can immediately be recognised.

This resulted in only one shift of controllers instead of three. In addition, instead of having three bases which each housed police officers and their vehicles and equipment, with the additional staff required in this one control room, an almost two thirds saving was achieved. Indeed, in time to come, the very existence of these police stations would be in jeopardy. But at what cost to police / public relations and the additional time it often took for responses to be made, was not well received by the public.

The problem arose when controllers with a good local knowledge of all three communities became few and far between, so the calls they received, for example, *"My bag has been stolen when I was in High Street"*, would need to be clarified as to which High Street the caller was referring to. In addition, there may well have been a spate of such thefts in the same area and indeed, the circumstances might even have thrown up likely suspects for such offences to those working in that particular control room. Such benefits were unlikely if the call referred to an area not so well known by the controller.

So in conclusion, I believe that nothing was more certain than the need to civilianise many of the roles not requiring the holder to possess a warrant card. However, I believe that the oil tanker was travelling too fast to have its brakes applied so that it stopped at a more practical distance and with sufficient consideration for the results. Indeed many of the larger police stations have since closed down completely and some have even merged with Fire Stations which makes the concept of 'Fire Brigade Policing' more of a reality! We have returned to those times when police officers were indeed employed as firemen also.

Surely, it is time for a re-think about such matters? The police have been robbed of the resources they require to do the job properly and if that wheel is ever replaced, it will now take a very long time to get the wheel tracking in proper balance and I sadly suspect that that will never be achieved.

17.

POLICE ACCOUNTABILITY

No matter how high ranking those in command of police forces reach, common sense dictates that there should always be some sort of independent arbiter or power in overall charge of their spending and practices, particularly of the type which the public might regard as a representation of themselves and their own communities.

Apparently, aptly named 'Watch Committees' formed in 1835 were the bodies who 'watched' over the police in that type of role. Subsequently, Police Authorities were formed by County Councils and their operation fell under the portfolio of what were termed 'Standing Joint Committees' of particular County Councils. From that, one correctly assumes that it was these county councils who at least paid a part in funding their police forces.

The modern-day Police Authority as I knew it consisted of a proportion of Magistrates and County Councillors from those counties in which the police were situated. My own 'West Mercia' force is a good example of a combined police authority which was made up with a proportion of councillors and magistrates from all of the constituent authorities.

Whilst this was never 100% satisfactory, the system appeared to work and the Chief Constable was regarded as in complete charge of the operational functions of his force but when taken to task, he was required to respond to the respective members of his Police Authority. I was asked on occasions to submit reports to the Chief in respect of operational issues which were fired at him by members of this Police Authority. This system was therefore the last system of its type before they were replaced by Police and Crime Commissioners who , more often than not, are from a 'political' background and who had lived and worked in one small area of the force.

At the time of writing, the Police Commissioner of the Metropolitan Police, Dame Cressida Dick is the only 'Chief of Police' of the type which were normally associated with previous warrant card holder heads of police forces.

It was Following the election of the Conservative–Liberal Democrat coalition in 2010, that an agreement was announced that: "We will introduce measures to make the police more accountable through oversight by a directly elected individual, who will be subject to strict checks and balances by locally elected representatives".

I suspect that the Government were of the opinion that Chief Constables had too much power and required closer supervision by someone or a body with no previous association with the police. (Some elected were indeed, retired Police Officers of senior ranks)

So it was that these new people and any small number of staff they wished to employ to assist them, were created by the Police Reform and Social Responsibility Act 2011 designed to replace police authorities in England and Wales. Exceptions were made in Greater Manchester and London where Police and Crime Commissioner (PCC) responsibilities are conducted by the mayors of those cities.

The first police and crime commissioners were elected in November 2012 and their responsibility was about the same as their predecessor Police Authorities. They were to be the voice of the people and hold the police to account, were responsible for the totality of policing with an aim to cut crime and deliver an effective and efficient police service within their force area.

The one huge difference here, is that this one person, would not be replacing Chief Constables but they were to be responsible for holding Chief

Constables and the force to account, effectively making the police answerable to the communities they serve. This is what Police Authorities did except that they were remote bodies of people, unpaid civil servants who were not present on a day-to-day basis, watching over the shoulder of the Chief Constable and his force. These commissioners now held the authority to appoint or sack their Chief Constable or in effect, fail to renew their contracts.

This consequently begged the question, "Who is in charge of the Police Force"? Is it the Chief Constable or the Police Commissioner?

There was indeed a scattering of so called 'Independent' applicants for these posts but almost without exception, most were sponsored by political parties or were members of them beforehand, some even being local councillors of particular political parties. This, in my view, was a huge black mark on the history of the police who, up until that time, had held party politics and their politicians at arm's length and were proud of it.

We were proud to be able to say that whilst the government of the day was in effect, our employer, we were not biased in any way to favour their party politics because, in any event, the members of Police Authorities represented a variety of different shades of party politics. The appointment of these politicians was in my view a huge backward step which witnessed the death of our previous independence from politics and politicians.

Every police force continues to have their chief officers comprising Deputy and Assistant Chief Constables, so who would those officers go to, should they wish to discuss matters with their boss?

It has been said that the Chief Constable is a person in charge of the Operational activities of their force, and specifically, not the PCC. However, as the nation has now witnessed on many occasions, we now have PCCs putting forward details of operational policing on nationwide media.

In conclusion, my view is that this change has represented one of the largest changes of shape to have affected the police service. I have not found anyone willing to support the view that this 'one person' PCC could adequately represent the communities of the vast areas, their police forces are asked to police today, and who have replaced what was a fairly representative group of people drawn from all of those counties concerned.

My distaste for such appointments also concerns the introduction of contracts designed when each Chief Officer is appointed. This immediately causes the Chief Officers concerned, to become obligated to their PCC. Surely they cannot criticise them when decisions are made contrary to their own views? Invariably, they want their contracts renewed, so which one of them would be brave enough to fall out of favour with their PCC?

Conversely, each PCC can elect to continue their office at election time, so when that is approached, it would be in the interest of PCCs to curry favour with their Chief Constables so that their support can be relied upon at election time. I hope by now, readers have come to the conclusion that I think that the replacement of Police Authorities with these 'one man band' politicians, stinks! – A very negative change of shape in more senses than one! Is it any wonder that at election time, voters have voted with their feet?

18.

INFORMATION TECHNOLOGY

When I retired as a Chief Superintendent on 28th November 1994, computing on a 'Personal Computer' (PC) had been in debate for some years within business circles in general. Not all were in favour of them and I can recall a few years prior to then, a very close friend of mine, a director of a large company supplying scientific apparatus to schools, who suggested that some offices were installing them as they thought it was the fashion. They were wondering what to do with them. These machines were certainly not on issue generally within Police Forces, but were in the process of being utilised. The jury on their usefulness was still out.

Many years later and having surpassed my thirty-year full pension date, I had been invited to join the Automatic Fingerprint Recognition Consortium (AFRC) which, as fate dictated, its 'Project Office' was a short walk away from my office at force headquarters, Hindlip Hall.

The process of my interview with the project manager was that I was to have dinner with him. He was from Hampshire and I had not met him before he walked into the Chinese restaurant where we were to dine. No doubt he wanted to look me over before offering me a contract. I made sure that I was there before him.

We ate a good Chinese meal but he was to floor me during it when he said, "Of course, being such a diverse organisation representing 37 different police forces, you will receive all of your work by e-mail and you will respond by the same means.

I wasn't aware then that each fingerprint bureau had been issued with a PC on which emails were exchanged with the project office. As pleased as I was to learn that I would become part of the team which rolled out the first computerised fingerprint storage and searching facility in England and Wales, the biggest shock was that right there and then, at the dinner table, I wasn't exactly sure what e-mail was, but I glibly responded, "Oh that shouldn't be a problem".

That friend who had wondered if PCs would take off in business, was a fellow Rotarian and even at the time when I was given that contract, we knew that not one of our forty odd members possessed an email address and probably not a PC. It's still remarkable now that although PCs started to become popular in 1978, this was 1994 and they really hadn't become a household product among the masses, let alone my family and friends.

The irony was, that during my last pre-inspection of the West Midlands Police in 1986 or 87, I learned that resulting from the sale of many police houses, the force had purchased sufficient PCs to equip all of their Sub Divisional commanders.

Dr. Tony Butler, the Chief Superintendent in charge of the project and who later retired as the Chief Constable of Gloucestershire, told me that they would be a tremendous help in disseminating training modules and would help the commanders to keep track of best practice etc.

Unfortunately, my few trips to Sub Divisions taught me that most of these Superintendents were old dogs who weren't that happy about learning new tricks. Many of their 'new issue' PCs had been securely locked up in cupboards in their offices. However, in the context of this story, I remained oblivious of their true worth, as did the HMI who I think was as ignorant about them as I was.

So, back to my story and my enjoyment of a Chinese meal with the AFR's Project Manager, Patrick (Pat) Pitt. I drove home still not sure what email was. I knew it was a form of messaging with the use of a computer, but the details were foreign to me. I arrived home and Jo wasn't that pleased that I was about to make quite a considerable purchase when I told her that in the morning, we were going to town to buy one.

Readers may not be surprised to learn that this purchase was probably the best one that I had ever made up until that day. I thoroughly enjoyed learning how to use it and it never ceased to amaze me how useful it was. That was 27 years ago and I can honestly say that every penny that I have earned during that time would not have been made had I not flattened out a steep learning curve through intense study and computer skill lessons.

Of course, some would argue that they could do without the long and many emails they receive from me but I'm well aware that my life has been completely led, if not vastly changed, as a result of my computer skills. I was proud to be the first Rotarian in our club to be able to operate one and when the second 'computerised' Rotarian appeared, we were able to 'blag' the rest of the club that we had joined a new 'On Line' Rotary Club organised in such a way, that all we had to do was to log on at a specific time so that we could conduct our business and, most importantly, earn an attendance tick.

My partner in computing happened to be a graphic artist and he produced a fake frontice piece which could be applied to any subject matter circulated among its 'fake' members.

Of course, purely for their information, he printed out a copy which he physically circulated to those among us at one of our meetings. Yes, you would be surprised to learn that most believed it and those that didn't were merely questioning it. How things have now moved on.

So what has all this got to do with the changes within our Police Service? I've drivelled on with this back cloth, purely to compare the differences of the 'then and now' eras as to how important messages can be disseminated quickly to those who should need to know the contents. As much as these machines have been a godsend and are truly magnificent in what they can do and increase the speed and ease of communicating with each other, there have been setbacks which I believe have been caused by them.

I have already described in my earlier 'Police Methods of Operation' Chapter, the system used in my early days in Herefordshire.- To recap, the 'B22' message forms filed on a small accessible pad.

The system was later improved when 'Telex' systems were introduced which comprised punched out tape converted from type which was then fed into a machine and sent to wherever the message was required to be received. These messages both in email form and other messages in transit were in the 'soft copy' form until printed out to become 'hard copies'.

The point which hopefully is now self-evident is that the PCs now have to be interrogated or the information held by them, printed off in order to see them. There cannot be any doubt about how more efficient our modern-day computerised systems are compared with those early days. For a start, all forces will have their own 'Intranet' system as well as the 'World Wide Web' Internet advantages on offer. It was West Mercia's Intranet system I learned to access so that I could analyse the Crime reporting and investigative processes. I later became familiar with additional 'Misper' software so that I could help to instruct the force on its use in connection with 'Missing Persons' enquiries.

So whilst these systems are clearly more efficient, my contention is that their use must be strictly monitored to ensure that adequate policing coverage is given to those who should be protected by their local force. The huge and obvious difference is that computers need to be accessed to obtain the necessary information intended to be shared. Compared to the old message system which meant that all one had to do in times past, was to read the messages. It has now, however, become necessary to rely on officers being able to use the machine to access the information themselves.

In addition, all reports will now be completed on computers and whilst tremendous strides in the technology have been made which results in computer access being available away from stations and even in vehicles, it is in the stations that most of the administration work is completed, which necessarily draws officers away from street duty and visibility.

My first computerised 'Crimes Analysis' was conducted at Kidderminster Police Station and I was horrified at what I was to discover. It was plainly obvious that the constables were receiving little or no supervision in their computer skills and in the operational work which would have been expected of them. Quite a proportion of beat officers and some of their supervisors, were not fully acquainted with their force's systems.

In effect, the blind supervisors were leading the blind and to be quite honest, I felt a sadness upon the realisation of this sorry state of affairs. It revealed that although the systems were fine, sometimes because information was 'out of sight' it was out of mind.

I have hopeful anticipation that as time progresses, the state of affairs will be improving all the time. It was then, however, necessary to tread very softly, softly with the Sergeants because this was where the supervision was lacking. Some of it would be down to their lack of computer literacy, but most of it was down to their lack of experience coupled with poor supervisory skills. I hasten to add now, that this was the situation I found around 10 years after their introduction; an era when most would have learned computer skills at school. But even those with the necessary skills were not being supervised in them or on the organisation of their use as a police tool.

So back then, I suddenly realised that we were now living with yet another generation of young inexperienced supervisors. It was no wonder that very often, all officers were found to be in the Police Station, tapping away at their computers.

Command and control systems were so efficient that I was able to find one example which, in addition to being able to prove that all operational officers on a shift were in the police station at the same time, also demonstrated the weakness of staff behind the enquiry desk and weak supervisory officers.

The example I have in mind occurred on one late evening when a father brought his 30-year-old or so son to the Police Station having discovered that his son had been fraudulently using his bank card to withdraw thousands of pounds from cash machines over a long period of time.

The father explained to the station duty office clerk the details of the fraud committed on him by his son. Unfortunately her command-and-control system then available to her led her to explain that there was no available police officer available to see them. (See previous on Civilianisation)

He waited around for about an hour and then left the Police Station with his son, who had already admitted to his father what he had done!

Subsequent enquiries with the 'Command and Control' computer, disclosed that every one of the police officers on duty at that time, were actually at the police station. Without anyone questioning the fact, they had all reported that they were there, report writing. As if this wasn't remarkable in itself, when I delved into the crime I found that the young officer who eventually recorded the crime did so under the category of the theft of a 'Credit Card' to the nominal value of 14 pence.

She had ignored the thousands of pounds that had been extracted from the account over a long period! For a start it was not a theft of the card because the son had no intention to permanently deprive his father of it. Indeed, after each time he used it, he put it back where he had found it.

The young officer hadn't realised that there was a specific offence of stealing from machines or meters. I couldn't blame her for that, though common sense should have dictated otherwise. Had she learned her definitions parrot fashion as previously mentioned many chapters ago, maybe she would have realised it. Apart from the training regime she may have been under, the major blame lay on those supervising such enquiries and I mention this purely as an example of one of many similar problems I had discovered.

As if to rub further salt into the wound, by the time the crime had eventually been recorded properly, the son had gone on the run. He had indeed, been arrested in another Police area but because the officer had failed to record the suspect as wanted on the Police National Computer, this crime and the fact that the son was wanted for it, never got picked up.

Many problems of similar levels were discovered in most divisions and I was beginning to make a name for myself. (Good and Bad) Many crimes recorded should have been written off as 'No Crimes' and, of course, writing them off would have caused the detection rates to increase. So, whilst the improved information technology receives a huge tick from me, the operational skills and changes required to ensure that information is not lost in these valuable machines and that they are used to enhance efficiency and not drown it, must be constantly monitored.

19.

CONCLUSIONS

There are a couple of proverbs which come to mind about how time flies by so quickly and money being the root of all evil.

It has taken my research into this book to realise that money has been behind many of the adverse effects on our policing. Little did I know then, that in 1967, the introduction of what was hailed as the great new system of 'Unit Beat Policing' would lead to the death of community policing as it was known, since time immemorial.

There's no doubt that the issue of personal radios and panda cars represented some of the most massive changes of shape in the history of modern policing. With the loss of village, estate constables and urban foot patrols, policing was to suddenly change from working the beat, to responding to incidents. 'Fire Brigade Policing' rolled off many tongues and 'response cars' in many forms followed.

The concept of Resident Beat Officers living on the estates which needed policing the most, was slain because of the effects of that system coupled with the lack of resources that forces needed to be able to sustain that excellent method of policing those areas.

Then, as if to rub salt into the wound, their vacant police houses were no longer required and were sold off for 'once in a lifetime' bounties to help money strapped forces balance their budgets.

The same applied to our village police stations with the advances in police mobility and communications seeing rural folk lose their beloved beat bobbies. People in places of power never considered that these advances would cause local village people such a huge loss and that nothing could replace the 'face to face' contact with a known constable, who was very often their friend as well as the guardian of peace and tranquillity.

Long gone and forever more, they were to be replaced by police anonymity and the sight of a police vehicle passing through their villages ----'If they were lucky'! They were very quickly to learn that technological advances are not always the 'be and end all' of better policing.

It was in this same year of 1967 when the four forces now comprising the West Mercia Constabulary were amalgamated. From the requirement to have four sets of Chief Officers to one singular set, the three other teams of Chief Officers were 'put out to grass'. It didn't, of course, stop there. Only one Police Headquarters was required and all the resources would now be centred at one place. Tremendous savings would have been made in many different facets, but at what cost and were those changes sustainable over time?

With Scotland now having just one police force and Wales only four, the idea of 'Regional' forces in England was discussed but packed away for the time being. I have little doubt that the idea of such regionalisation will be revisited by this, or future governments in their blinded notions to save even further resources.

As if they were blinded by the results of such actions, the cancer continued to grow. With having already cast village and estate policing to the sword, they looked towards our urban centres of commerce and population. Yes, they were next in line.

A recent investigation by a national newspaper disclosed that around 50% of our remaining police stations with front counters where the public can talk to officers have closed in the past 2010-2020 decade. That amounts to a massive 667 police stations!

The 'Freedom of Information' questions received responses from 39 of the 43 forces and indicates that fewer than 600 police stations are now open to the public. The responses have indicated that cities including Bath, St Albans and Ely no longer have any dedicated stations with front counters. London's Metropolitan Police "has lost 106 stations and now has just 36 after selling off £1bn worth of property".

My very recent interview of a Community Police Support Officer, (CPSO), Denise Bushell, from the town of Droitwich, quite surprised me because the comparatively modern police station building with a Magistrates Court attached was still being used as a base for a police team but the Magistrates' Court no longer functioned as such and the front desk at the Police Station ceased to operate as a public service.

My surprise was compounded when I learned that in her police team, there was just one sergeant, three police officers and five CPSOs. This was a Police Station in which I had worked as a Sergeant and Inspector. It was also later under my command as a Superintendent and Chief Superintendent. The new police station was built not far from the old one which gave way to the building of a supermarket and its car park. It was then big enough to host a police club and had quite a large car park. I worked at both police stations.

The old police station was in the centre of a row of police houses, some being used as single quarters for probationary constables. On the other side, the Magistrates Clerk's office and the court were located. Both stations had a number of village police stations and resident officers with a core of police officers working shifts around the clock. It had its own control room from where the personnel were directed.

The current population of 23,000 are now required to travel 6.5 miles to Worcester should they want to see a police officer in person or report some lost or found property. I cannot believe that the need for community contact with the police has diminished to such an extent; to the contrary, in reality the need will have increased in line with the rise in crime.

But of course, the lack of available police services will be reflected in the reduction of the need to report information or seek such services. If no police are around to report such things, the demand for their services will inevitably decrease. The powers that be, will most likely suggest that crimes and other incidents have decreased – of course they will, as there is no-one to report them to and the public will not be bothered to have to report things to a police station which is anywhere other than in its own community.

Feeling the pressure, numerous defensive statements have been made by Chief Officers who appear to be pressured by those holding the purse strings into arguing that people don't use police stations the way they once did and that nowadays, a small proportion of crimes are reported at police front counters.

That may be so, but public counters at police stations greet many members of the public whose visits may not be for that purpose. I have done that job and even then, back in the 1970s, most queues in police stations were for a multitude of other problems, and very few were to report crimes which were normally reported on the telephone. Indeed, a recent survey indicates that only around 25% of the crimes reported are reported through physical visits to police stations.

The very presence of a police station will always be welcomed by the community it serves, so why can't the powers that be, see that? They can only see the financial benefits in not providing such resources and not the benefits of the people they are supposed to serve and protect.

In addition, those police stations now lost, will have contained many officers who were hitherto, responsible for policing the community in that same area. Where have they all gone? Is it thought by those in the communities that they've left behind, that they will travel from where they are now, back to those areas to perform their policing function? What do you think?

For a start, they may not even exist at all because the loss of every police station will amount to the easing of police budgets at the expense of the prevention and detection of crime. Others taken from community policing will have been creamed off into specialist roles which weren't necessary in days gone by.

We are beginning, no, we have already begun to fail in the duties of a constable as defined in the definition recorded many chapters above. Not to mention Prime Minister Theresa May who personally reduced 20,000 police officers 'at a stroke'. The government purse strings have foolishly been cut, when at a time, it was necessary for their funding to be kept up with demand.

Forces including the Met have launched online crime-reporting services and developed ridiculed schemes such as 'virtual police officers' as if to make them a replacement for real police officers. Such are most definitely ineffective when compared to the reassurance offered by face-to-face contact and the privacy of a police station.

With money being the root of at least, most evil, the root of the problem can be found in the conclusions drawn from the 2018 Public Accounts Committee report which found that "forces are selling off more of their assets to try and raise some funds for capital investment and increasingly drawing on their reserves". So, the family silver continues to disappear.

The appointments of full time Police Commissioners and their staff must have absorbed an annual drain on those finances. Although police income is received from a variety of channels, it is still mostly the Home Office Grants and Local Authority taxes which, in the main fund the service which, by the way, is the same pot that feeds the budgetary requirements of our Police and Crime Commissioners.

This so-called phenomenon for them to act as a conduit for improved police / community relationships has proved to be a double whammy because, on the one hand, they provide a huge cost to the already finance strapped police budgets to exist and on the other hand, their objective of being that conduit was always bound to fail, because it is impossible for one person to reach out to all of the communities which hitherto were at least, represented by their own 'Police Authority' membership for the areas in which they were living and representing.

We now see on TV, well-meaning people in civilian clothes, mostly from political backgrounds, as PCCs, putting out the message to the public on various aspects of operational policing. This is a subject which they had no or little prior involvement or experience with and they should cease to pretend by their actions that they are acquainted with it.

These people don't look the part, nor should they try to play the part. It is the Chief Officer of Police who is responsible for the operational policing of the force and by comparison, don't they look smart and fit for purpose when they do?

With Chief Officers being on short term contracts and with their commissioners having the power to sack them, this has become a recipe for disaster because the Chiefs have had their legs cut from beneath them to open the gates of political power in the police service. So working under the shadow of these commissioners and being anxious to renew their contracts, what Police Chief will have the nerve to speak out or otherwise upset his commissioner? One wonders when it will be that one of these two so called 'heads of the police' will disappear for the sake of the further squeezing of police budgets.

It is the dramatic change to the efforts expended in the detection of crime process that brings me the most sadness. 'The Job' was always regarded as a vocation involving the challenge of catching criminals and seeing those criminals put behind bars or otherwise brought to justice. Yet, resulting from the 'own goals' scored by a tiny minority of our members, I discover that it's no longer 'The Job'' but has now become simply 'A Job' without being drawn to it by a sense of vocation and now occupied by many members just for the financial rewards at the end of the month.

Yes, like 99.99% of police employments, we must not abuse our authority but tying the hands of the police behind their backs and blindfolding them to the extent that is now apparent, almost guarantees their freedom unless they confess their wrongdoings. It just isn't fair to our communities and above all, those unfortunate victims who have suffered at the wrongdoers hands.

So, it is this situation which has shrunk the level of motivation held in my day, to detect crime and capture criminals. I have no doubt that all plugs will still be pulled to capture the authors of heinous crimes such as murder, rapes and offences against children but the everyday lawlessness of the petty thief, burglar or thug will continue to grow unabated with their knowledge that with cops not bothering to arrest them because of the known outcome, in possessing far better chances than was ever known, of simply 'getting away with it'.

Whilst not doubting that camaraderie still exists in police stations, to what extent compared with days gone by, is impossible to measure but I'm constantly being told that job satisfaction has dropped to an all-time low. The excitement or the desire to catch criminals has now waned. The hammer used has proved to be far too big to crack that nut.

My research with officers from Avon and Somerset, tells me that whilst morale is high among new officers, who seem to be full of energy and enthusiasm, longer serving officers are feeling more worn out. There is no longer an appetite for 'overtime working' which, during my research, was said to be a real sign that people are tired and value their time off away from work. On the question of the closure of police clubs, a senior supervisor informed me that she really enjoyed a drink post shift but that is now a distant memory for most and because police clubs were all closed a long time ago, many have never experienced the camaraderie which they generated.

In response to my questions concerning having 'fun on the job' I was informed that the demand was so high and resources so stretched, people don't have time for fun. No 'down time' is experienced and often refreshments are being taken in front of laptops, not even giving themselves a break for a laugh over their refreshments.

So just imagine that someone very close to you has been raped or that the privacy of your home has been invaded by some 'yob' or 'yobs' who have made a right mess of it. All this, purely with the intention of taking money or goods, very often heirlooms or objects of sentimental value from you, just to feed their greed or more likely their drug using habits. I'm sure minds can conjure that picture.

The police will be alerted and hopefully attend and make enquiries. Their response to rapes will hopefully be immediate as it should be with burglaries and all other crimes, however, due to lack of resources, some forces have applied screening procedures which have even ruled out the police attendance at petty burglaries where the value of property stolen has been below a certain ceiling.

On the other hand, even on those occasions when, through advances in forensic science, or even when the culprits may have been named by a third party, they may be left to fight a battle with the Crown Prosecution Service whose remit of reducing court backlogs hangs like the sword of Damocles over their solicitors' heads.

But even before those agencies become alerted, you may well be told that because the suspect could only be held for a limited period without being charged, that they have had to release him or her. Clearly those responsible for this type of legislation have never had to battle against the clock to gather evidence. Credible witnesses will be away from home, scientists will be unable to forensically examine exhibits and report the results in good time and a mountain of other obstacles are put into investigators' paths.

Being unable to overcome those obstacles and thus push these mountains aside, has caused motivation to crumble and all this tends to result in suspects not being arrested so early in the process. Indeed, they may never get arrested at all so that they remain free to carry on in whatever dastardly deeds they may have been involved in .

So, all the weights in the balancing pan of criminal justice are such which might inevitably work in favour of suspects, in them being arraigned in courts and eventually, 'off the hook'. But let's imagine that all has gone well and some good circumstantial evidence exists to put the suspect/s well into the frame of guilt. "All we need now is the slightest of coughs" you might say. (A cough is police parlance for an admission.)

And so, on arrest, he or she is clearly told the reasons for their arrest, but before they ask any questions, the suspect is advised that he need not answer those questions........**WHAT!**

Yes, WHAT on earth has gone wrong? For whatever reason, it appears that since the caution contains the advice that suspects do not have to say anything and that this concept has been seen time and again on television, they can, and more often than not do, merely sit there and fail to say anything at all, apart from, of course – 'NO COMMENT'.

The full wording of the caution is :-

"You do not have to say anything. But it may harm your defence if you do not mention when questioned something which you later rely on in court. Anything you do say may be given in evidence."

The words, "You do not have to say anything" have always been contained within the caution but now, it includes the advice that their defence may be harmed if they do not mention anything which they later rely upon in court. However, they will have been advised by their legal representative, not to say anything. Of course, what it doesn't say is that if your suspect does answer any of their questions, they might drop themselves right in the mire!!

So, if you were a solicitor, what would you advise your client to do?

Normally, our defendants in court are far from smart people but whatever their intellect, they are smart enough to know that it is up to the prosecution to prove their case beyond reasonable doubt and how the cookie crumbles when being interviewed is best dealt with by saying nothing.

The effects of this huge shape of change were never seen coming because harming their defence in court may, of course, never happen because they stand a far better chance of not arrive in court without the police getting their cough in the first place!

BUT HANG ON; these are people who, following police enquiries, are suspected of committing maybe the simplest and maybe the most heinous and sometimes, horrific of crimes against society. Surely they should be made to answer the questions posed by the police? Ok, the responses received stand a good chance of denials or lies but **WHAT ISN'T FAIR ABOUT THAT?** The positive to be taken is that their accounts given can be investigated which might lead to their release or being charged.

Suspects are or usually are, a lot more involved than ordinary witnesses who may have been interviewed and have provided statements as to their knowledge about the crimes being investigated. Suspects are people where at least some shred of evidence exists to suggest that they may be responsible for the offence. It is for that reason that they have been arrested so why shouldn't they answer the questions put to them by the police who are investigating the crime? Surely, if they are not guilty of the crime and have nothing to hide, they ought to simply answer the questions which should ensure their release from custody. What have they got to lose?

One could probably guess that this was a human rights issue. The concept of the right to silence is simply advising the suspects that they are not obliged to help the police but it is not specifically mentioned in the European Convention of Human Rights but the European Court of Human Rights has held that: -

the right to remain silent under police questioning and the privilege against self-incrimination are generally recognised international standards which lie at the heart of the notion of a fair procedure under Article 6.

So this, in my view, especially the 'No Comment' answer interviews we witness on TV, have been the cause of justice being unfairly swamped in this unfair 'Human Rights' issue. If there ever was a pendulum which in theory, should swing towards justice being equal to all, then it has swung far more than it ought to, in favour of the accused. (How many times have I said that?)

It is my heartfelt view that this sorry state of affairs can only encourage those who wish to commit crime, to commit further crimes. The balancing pan weighs so heavily in their favour. How on earth our lawmakers have allowed this to happen, heaven knows but we should move heaven and earth to put it right.

One thing is certain; there is no way on earth which can dictate that a suspect be forced to answer questions. To do that, I have pictures of torture in mind, and of course, we shan't tread there!

However, what I have in mind is a far heavier reliance on that part of the caution which states:- **But it may harm your defence if you do not mention when questioned something which you later rely on in court.**"

Having now witnessed many of these interviews it appears that the justification by solicitors to advise their clients to make 'No Comment' interviews rely on the fact that the evidence, as weak as it may be, has not been declared by the police. So let us include the evidence within the question.

I will deal with that concept in more depth below but first, let me explore some of the 'Case Law' which was discussed on the right of silence and which occurred in the years leading up to the Police and Criminal Evidence Act of 1984.

The decisions made can be best summarised in an article on the subject contained from **The Law Society Gazette dated 2nd December 1987.**

This article contained discussion on many stated cases but I have taken the liberty of summarising the main ingredients and hopefully without any bias on the subject. Some passages I have copied in their entirety and others I have summarised.

Justice Melford Stevenson, known as the outspoken judge had given a direction to a jury to draw an inference of guilt from the belated accused's explanation when in court and not when interviewed by the police.

He directed that the belatedness of the explanation could be a factor to be taken into account when assessing its weight. His deductions went against him because it was held that the accused exercised his right to remain silent and the jury could take his silence into account whichever way they wanted to.

Numerous case law was used to bat the argument both ways and its importance here is that the final straws of debate no doubt shaped the Police and Criminal Evidence Act of 1984. (PACE)

The view taken by the Court of Criminal Appeal in one case was that, as the accused was told that he was not obliged to say anything, it would be a trap for him if the jury were invited to draw an adverse inference from his silence. The Criminal Law Revision Committee ('CLRC') were in no doubt that the rule that an invitation to draw an inference of guilt from the accused's silence was a misdirection.

It was rightly said, in my view, that the caution merely serves to remind the accused of a right which he already possesses in common law. This was after an exhaustive review of the authorities both judicial and academic, when the court concluded that there were no rules of law that an inference of guilt could never properly be drawn in a criminal trial from the silence of a suspect when being questioned by the police.

The courts were in effect therefore, falling back on the old position in that what in normal circumstances precluded such an inference was the giving of a caution (i.e. it would amount to a trap if, being cautioned, his resulting silence could be held against him). I would have added, "OK, let's do away with the caution altogether". Some hope I know, but.....

Yet, it was said, the caution was never a requirement of law; merely a rule of prudence designed to ensure the admissibility of confessions and advised by the judges in extra-judicial pronouncements. Reference was then made of the Chief Constable of Birmingham's letters asking whether or not differing interpretations received by his officers were correct or not. One judge had castigated an officer for giving the caution and another had criticised an officer for not giving it.

The way forward has now resulted in the Police and Criminal Evidence Act 1984 which perpetuates the caution and to some extent upgrades its status compared with the Judges' Rules in that under Section 67 any new draft code must be approved by a resolution of both Houses of Parliament. The original caution was subsequently amended to add that their case may be harmed if they failed to give an explanation which subsequently be used in their defence.

However, it had been stated that having examined numerous case law on the subject, The Home Secretary need only introduce a revised code with the caution deleted, and in obtaining the necessary approval, he could reassure parliamentarians that no fundamental common law basis for retaining it was at stake, because in a case of ' Chandler' the court expressly said there was none.

It was deduced that with the caution gone, an inference of guilt from silence would then become permissible, subject in general to the meticulous process of reasoning which the court stipulated in some 'Case Law'. In one such case it was declared - *'Undoubtedly, when persons are speaking on **even terms**, and a charge is made, and the person charged says nothing, and expresses no indignation, and does nothing to repel the charge, that is some evidence to show that he admits the charge to be true.'*

So, the words**, speaking 'on even terms'** now became a really important statement and it was suggested that if an accused had a solicitor present at an interview or if the interview were to be tape recorded, then this interview would be regarded as being 'on even terms'. It was a broad principle of common sense. The real issue in the whole debate over the right of silence is guaranteeing the suspect's access to legal advice rather than senior policemen in the witness box blithely offering spurious grounds for denying it.

It was suggested that it would be straining the concept of **'even terms'** if a suspect were to be denied the presence of a solicitor. However, what of the position when a solicitor advises his client to say nothing? It was suggested that any prospect of an adverse inference can be effectively negated by the simple solicitors strategy of not wanting his client to say anything until he was made aware of the full evidence against his client.

In those circumstances, it was thought advisable to discourage any responses until substantial details of the prosecution case had been disclosed. In other words, the defence didn't want the fairness to sway away from them until they knew what cards the police held, when of course, they could put forward their version of events and maybe 'trump' the police's cards they played.

This is the area which I believe could be further explored to attack the 'No Comment' interviews, which, in anyone's language, is far removed from fairness or common sense.

Should we now ask the questions by first disclosing the reason for the question and the evidence in support of it. A simple example might be: – The suspect has been seen by a witness to be in the area of the murder at the pertinent time, 10pm.

So, instead of the question being framed – "Where were you at 10pm?" Why not ask, "We have a witness, your neighbour who saw you there at 10pm. Do you agree with that and if not, where were you"?

Why should a defendant not answer any such or similar questions? I would add that not giving the rationale for our questions has always been like playing a game of poker. We now serve every shred of evidence on the defence (albeit for committal purposes) whereas years ago, prior to the Criminal Justice Act, we didn't, so what is to be lost?

The police could also continually repeat the warning contained in the caution that "**it may harm your defence if you do not mention when questioned something which you later rely on in court**". It appears to me that the meaning of that statement is not forced home hard enough, not just at the caution stage, but right throughout the questioning of suspects. I am convinced that this is an area which might just cause that pendulum to swing more in the direction of Justice! Let's start to get the wheels of justice back on – please!

20.

ACKNOWLEDGEMENTS

I am indebted to many past and current police officers, PCSOs and other lawyers and friends of the justice arena in which we have often fought our legal battles.

In particular, those ladies who once adorned their smart uniforms at times when they were once defined as 'specialist' women officers and in more modern times when they served on shift with their male colleagues. In particular, Jean Mulcaster, Julie Lloyd (now Rees) and Jackie Bristow (now Perkins). It was also Jackie who so kindly invited myself and two other old police dinosaur members of the past 'Retained Experienced Personnel' scheme, for a gorgeous Sunday lunch over which we spent some time discussing the diversity issues relating to their employment.

Thanks also in a similar vein to Senior Police and Community Support Officer, Denise Bushell who provided me with a glimpse into her daily routine in support of the local community policing team she now works with in the town of Droitwich Spa.

With regard to more modern-day policing, I must also thank Chief Inspector Jessica Aston of the Avon and Somerset Local Policing Area (LPA) the Commander for North Somerset- Weston Super Mare who was able to provide me with an up-to-date appreciation concerning the morale and camaraderie of her officers in comparison with those of the recent past.

Also, in furtherance of such comparisons, particularly with community initiatives, I am also very thankful to former Chief Superintendent Richard James, now carrying out advisory support to police and local authorities with a focus on developing and implementing effective local policing, using evidence-based techniques. His appraisal of the challenges of neighbourhood policing from the perspective of police and community support officers and his development into a training programme for PCSOs and neighbourhood policing teams, has been most helpful.

To proof reader, Ian Johnston, now a retired Detective Superintendent who, as an Inspector, I involved in the leadership of a merry band of officers in a team called 'The West Mercia Task Force' all of whom served with great distinction, success and camaraderie. Ian led the investigation into the so called 'Road Rage' murder in Worcestershire when Tracey Andrews was convicted of the murder of her fiancé, Lee Harvey in July 1997 and given life imprisonment. He also became a colleague when, following our retirements, we both worked in the 'Retained Experienced Personnel' team in West Mercia. I asked him to be ruthless in his proofreading – and he was. Thanks Ian.

My grateful thanks also go to Eric Kent who I first met 43 years ago when I was a Detective Sergeant working at Halesowen in the West Midlands. Eric was our new neighbour and in my opinion, a very skilled cartoonist. It was Eric who designed the cover of this book. He has been retired for around 20 years and has tirelessly worked for children's charities in his retirement.

In addition and finally, I thank all those people, including my golfing, bowling and table tennis mates who, as far as I'm aware, have never fallen foul of the law or police officers, but who are always willing to give me their opinions on how they would put things right!

Printed in Great Britain
by Amazon